The Amazing
Lost Money-Secret
of the U.S.
Government

by
J. Andrew Douglas

TABLE OF CONTENTS

CHAPTER XIV

INTRODUCTION
WHAT'S IN IT FOR YOU?

If you read this book carefully and use the information properly, you will be getting money from the U.S. Government. In some cases the amount you receive will be sizeable. Perhaps you'll be receiving checks monthly. It's up to you.

Read each chapter. The book is divided into sections by departments of the government or independent agencies. Each of these departments or agencies has money available for the asking. In each section, in addition to an explanation of the services offered, is a list of programs under which you may be eligible for cash from the government. At the end of each section is a directory of addresses and phone numbers of each department's regional and headquarter's office.

Here are just a few examples of people who can collect money from the government. If you are a farmer, student, artist, longshoremen or harbor worker there are funds for you. Families and children, the blind or disabled, and veterans may all receive government benefits. If you need money to start a business or to get an education the

Government has the money to help you. There are ways to collect Social Security no matter what your age. Retired Senior Volunteers can get money. There is money for loans of all kinds - agricultural, housing, and natural resource. No matter what your need read this book and contact these government agencies, ask about their programs, let them send you pamphlets for your use and information. It's your government, they are there to help you. They cannot seek you out so you must be aware of what they have to offer and get it.

No matter what your circumstance if you want to buy a new home or repair your old one, return to school, get care for a handicapped relative, get a loan to start a business or cover losses suffered because of a natural disaster.

If your particular question is not answered here, the address and phone number of someone who can answer you is included in this book.

Here are some tips for you when calling or writing for information:

1) Have a specific question in mind when you call or write. It will save you time. Vague questions will get vague answers.

2) Call the phone number listed for information.

3) You will rarely need the top administrator, therefore you won't need the name of the director. There are frequent changes in personnel so the name is not important.

4) What is important? The name of the office or organization. Keep it in mind when calling.

5) When writing include the name of the office, organization or program. Your letter will be given to a person who can answer your questions.

CHAPTER I

U.S. DEPARTMENT OF HEALTH, EDUCATION, AND WELFARE

WHAT IS THE DEPARTMENT OF HEALTH, EDUCATION AND WELFARE?

In 1953 the Department of Health, Education and Welfare was established as an elevation of the Federal Security Agency. Of all the domestic departments it has the largest budget. In all, it administers about 250 programs. The oldest is the Public Health Service hospitals which was established in 1798. The health activities of the department were greatly expanded through legislation in the 1960's.

The greatest part of the department's budget, almost 90%, goes to the states in the form of grants in aid to match or supplement State and local spending for health, education and welfare programs and to colleges,

1

universities, hospitals, and scientific institutions as grants for research and training programs.

To improve our health this department offers grants in aid for pollution and construction of waste control treatment works. It supports research studies to aid in discovering new treatment and ultimately the prevention or cure of the major illnesses of man. The department assists medical schools with financial and consultative help in addition to offering fellowships, internships, and residencies. Through the Food and Drug Administration it preserves the purity and safety of foods, drugs, and cosmetics. Handicapped persons as well as needs of special groups are served through this department.

The office of Education is also under the Department of H.E.W. It administers and seeks to improve education through guidance programs granting funds so some may improve their education. The educational needs of the mentally retarded, emotionally disturbed, and physically handicapped are met through this department.

The welfare of citizens is a concern of the Department of H.E.W. and is met by such programs as Social Security and Vocational Rehabilitation as well as the Civil Defense Emergency Services.

HOW CAN I GET MONEY FROM THE DEPARTMENT OF HEALTH, EDUCATION AND WELFARE?

The regional offices are listed in the directory in this book, as well as the phone number and address of the national headquarters office. Whatever your need, these sources will be capable of answering your questions.

If your need money for any of the following the Department of H.E.W. can help you through one of its 250 programs.

Do you want to become qualified to work even if you're handicapped?

Do you want money to go to school to become a doctor?

Are you blind or disabled, physically or mentally, or over 65 and need money to live?

Do you need more food for your family?

These and many other financial questions are answered in detail in the next section. You can get money now if you are eligible for these programs. Read on and find out exactly how.

DEPARTMENT OF HEALTH, EDUCATION, AND WELFARE

Public Assistance. This program is offered through The Social and Rehabilitation Service. It provides financial aid to states for aid to families with dependent children, emergency welfare assistance, assistance to repatriated U.S. Nationals, and in Guam, Puerto Rico, and the Virgin Islands aid to the aged, blind permanently, and totally disabled and the administration of these welfare programs.

Money is paid directly to eligible families by states. These families are needy aged, blind, disabled, or families with dependent children and use the money for food, shelter, clothing, and other necessary items of daily living. Payments in the form of money or vendor payments assist these families in crisis situations, such as eviction or lack of food.

In 1973 fiscal year, about 14 million different recipients received maintenance assistance, in 1974 and 1975 there were 14,300,000 and 11,400,000 respectively.

There are other related programs which include The Medical Assistance Program, Rehabilitation Services and Facilities - Basic Support, Public Assistance - Social

Services, Social Security - Disability Insurance and Supplemental Security Income.

For additional or specific information contact your local welfare agency.

The headquarters office may also be contacted for further information:

Office of Public Information
Social and Rehabilitation Service
Department of Health, Education, and Welfare
Washington, D.C. 20201
(202) 245-0392

Public Assistance - Social Services. This agency provides those who now receive or may receive public assistance with other services which will enable them in attaining the least level of dependence on public welfare. These services will help them towards achieving employment and self-care.

Formula Grants are offered and may be used for proper and efficient operations of social service programs which are designed to obtain self-support and sufficiency. They also provide legal services, family planning services, information and help in home and money management, child care or protective services. Funds received are to be spent according to a federally approved state plan.

All states, the District of Columbia, Puerto Rico, the Virgin Islands, and Guam are eligible. In addition, any needy person who now receives or may receive welfare funds for blind, aged, permanently or totally disabled or a dependent child who meets State requirements are also eligible applicants.

In fiscal year 1974, about 6 million individuals received one or more social services under this program. Over 2 million individuals received services under the programs for the aged, blind, and disabled. During fiscal year 1975, these figures increased. 6,300,000 received services and 2,400,000 individuals received services under the program for the aged, blind, or disabled.

For more information contact:

> Community Service Administration
> Social and Rehabilitation Service
> 330 C Street
> Washington, D.C. 20201
> (202) 245-8717

IF YOU ARE AN AMERICAN RETURNING FROM A FOREIGN COUNTRY, YOU CAN GET MONEY FROM THE U.S. GOVERNMENT.

Temporary Assistance for Repatriates. If you are a United States citizen or the dependent of a U.S. citizen. Dependents may include spouse, parents, and children who are minors and unmarried, adopted, stepchildren, adult, unmarried children, who are handicapped.

Under this program, the Federal Government helps U.S. citizens who have become ill or run out of money while in a foreign country. When they are returned to this country because of illness or lack of money, the funds are available. No funds have been appropriated by Congress to assist in the maintenance of destitute or ill U.S. citizens while in a foreign country.

The program called Temporary Assistance for Repatriates, provides persons returned to the U.S. with money if they are not eligible for other income-maintenance programs like welfare. Money may also be provided if the person does not have funds readily available.

The funds may be used for food, shelter, transportation, clothing, and medical care. Even special services such as foster care for children may be covered by these funds.

As part of the assistance program these services may also be provided: counseling, gudiance, and vocational rehabilitation.

One requirement for eligibility is need, According to the Civil Rights Act of 1964, no regard to race, color or national origin may be made.

Public Law 86-571 in July 1960 grants assistance to U.S. citizens who are returned to this country because of mental illness.

To be eligible for assistance, you must be 1) a U.S. citizen or dependents of U.S. citizens and 2) in need. Need, as defined under this program, means you are actually living in the United States, having returned from a foreign country because you are destitute or ill, mentally or physically, or there is war or threat of war and you are without available resources for living expenses.

Any information given to the Public Welfare Agency is held in confidence.

Persons are identified as being qualified for aid under

this program by the U.S. Department of State. After returning to this country because you are ill or destitute the State Department notifies the Assistance Payments Administration in the Department of Health, Education, and Welfare about it. They are notified of your time and port of arrival. This information is obtained from the U.S. Counselor abroad.

A welfare worker will be sent to you and your family. These arrangements are made by the Assistance Payments Administration and the welfare agency in your state.

Such services as medical care, financial assistance, and counseling to aid you in reestablishing your family in the United States will be provided by the welfare worker.

If your port of entry is not your final destination, the welfare agency in the community in which you will live will assist you.

Other services which may be provided by the community welfare agency include child welfare, vocational or occupational training and services in renewing ties with relatives.

After you and your family become self-supporting, aid under this program ceases. There is, however, a limit to how long aid is provided. It is 13 months after you have arrived in the U.S. For severely handicapped, it is 19 months.

If you become eligible under another aid program for assistance, the aid under this program will stop.

At the time you are receiving aid any changes in circumstances which affect your eligibility must be reported immediately to the welfare agency.

You are expected to repay the government when you are able. Your welfare agency determines how much and the terms of repayment.

Money or other income that is necessary for self-support for you and your family is not considered as being an available source for repayment.

For more information:

> Assistance Payments Administration
> Social and Rehabilitation Service
> U.S. Department of Health, Education,
>   and Welfare
> 330 Independence Avenue S.W.
> Washington, D.C. 20201

Bureau of Family Services. This bureau administers five federally aided programs of public assistance. They include Old Age Assistance, Aid to the Permanently and Totally Disabled, Aid to the Blind, Aid to Families with Dependent Children, and Medical Assistance for the Aged. The Federal Government finances more than half the aid and medical care funds distributed through these programs.

Congress sets certain standards for the states to meet if they are to receive Federal aid for these programs. It is left to the state to determine eligibility requirements, what "proof of need" applicants must supply, and the amount of aid. The Bureau of Family Services also makes demonstration grants to State agencies.

Children's Bureau. According to its basic act of 1912, this bureau investigates conditions affecting all matters pertaining to child welfare. In addition, they seek to improve practices in child health and welfare programs.

The Children's Bureau by means of Federal grants-in-aid to State agencies assists in maternal and child health care, care for crippled children and other welfare services. Grants for training, research, and demonstration are made to State agencies, public, and nonprofit organizations and institutions.

Here are some things funds may be used for: 1) social workers trying to keep families together or working out problems of children, 2) improve training and number of social workers, 3) homemaker services, foster homes, adoption, other child welfare programs, 4) clinics, 5) public health nurses, 6) school health programs, 7) special clinics for mentally retarded, and 8) consultation and technical assistance to agencies concerned with the problems of youth.

What does all this mean to you? If you are a family with dependent children, you can get payments for medical, money for food, shelter, and clothing and help with family problems.

Aid to Families with Dependent Children may be claimed by children and their families who need money or medical care because a parent is dead, disabled, absent from home, or (in some states) unemployed.

To be eligible, need is the main factor. You don't have to be destitute or completely without money or resources. If you are in need, no matter what your race, color, or national origin, you are eligible.

Rules for Aid to Families with Dependent Children

vary from state to state. For instance, each state has its own eligibility rules. They decide how much a family needs for food, clothing, and shelter and how much the state can pay to help them.

In some states, children must stay in school if they are under 18, in order to be eligible to receive payments. Other variable factors include the length of time a family has lived in the state before they may receive aid and how long a parent must be gone before payments are received.

Medical care is covered in most states by paying the doctor bill.

Your local welfare agency can tell you whether or not you are eligible for aid. If you were not eligible in the past or in a different state, contact the agency and check again. Laws vary from state to state, and the Federal and State laws regarding aid change frequently.

All states follow these rules:

1) The state must accept an application for Aid to Families with Dependent Children from everyone who wants to apply.

2) They must write within 30 days of application to tell you how much you get paid or why you are not eligible.

3) Each state must make payments within 30 days to eligible families regardless of race, creed, color, or national origin.

4) They must also give anyone who asks for it an opportunity for a fair hearing.

If you have dependent children and do not have enough money for food, clothing, medical care, or a place to live, contact your nearest local welfare agency. They can help or find someone who can. Look it up in your local telephone directory.

Aid to the Blind. Grants to states for aid to the blind were provided in 1935 in Title X of the Social Security Act. The purpose of the program is to enable blind people, who are needy, to obtain the essentials of living and aid them in participating in community life. Through financial assistance, the Government aims to help the needy, blind achieve self-support or self-care.

Each state has its own rules for application and eligibility. To find out the specific requirements, contact your local welfare agency.

Aid to Disabled. Grants to states for aid to the disabled were provided in 1950 in Title XIV of the Social Security Act. Financial assistance to permanently and totally disabled is offered so they may achieve self-support or self-care, or to make the best use of their remaining ability.

Again, rules and requirements vary in each state. Find out those in your state by contacting your local welfare agency.

Funds for Aid to the Blind and Aid for the Permanently and Totally Disabled come partly from the U.S. Government so there are some rules that all states must follow:

1) The state must accept an application for Aid for the Permanently and Totally Disabled and Aid to the Blind from everyone who wants to apply.

2) They must write within 30 days of application to tell you how much you get paid or why you are not eligible.

3) Each state must make payments within 30 days to eligible familes regardless of race, creed, color, or national origin.

4) They must also give anyone who asks for it an opportunity for a fair hearing.

In order to obtain aid through either program, you just follow certain Federal rules for eligibility. Aid for the

Blind cannot be received until an eye examination by an optometrist or opthalmologist has been completed on the applicant. The agency usually pays for necessary eye examinations. A State supervisory opthalmologist makes a study of the report of your eye examination and a review team decides on your disability.

All income and resources are taken into account, however, allowances are made for expenses.

Blind persons attempting to become self-supporting by acquiring a skill may be allowed to earn money and use resources to carry out their plan without losing their eligibility. The time limit is 12 months. After that the agency disregards the first $85 of monthly income you earn and counts only one-half of the rest.

Your local welfare agency can assist you. They are listed in the telephone directory.

Supplemental Security Income. These benefits are available through the Social Security Administration to provide additional income to supplement Social Security Income to those 65 and older or to those who are blind or disabled. The disability may be mental or physical.

Payments are direct and unrestricted in use.

The eligibility of people 65 or over and blind or

physically or mentally disabled is determined on the basis of his resources and monthly income. For the purpose of determining income the first $20 of Social Security or other income would not be counted. An additional $65 of earned income plus one-half of any monthly earnings above $65 would also not be counted. If after this the individual's counted income is less than $146 per month and resources are less than $1,500 he is eligible. For a couple the amount per month, if they are both categorized as above, is $219, counted income and $2,250 in resources.

This includes savings accounts, stocks, bonds, jewelry and other valuables.

The things that do not count are as follows: your home, personal effects, such as household goods, if valued at $1,500 or less. Only the portion of the retail value exceeding $1,200 is counted. A car doesn't count at all if it is used for transportation to a job or to place for regular medical treatments.

If you live in someone else's home such as your son or daughter your payment will be less.

Eligible people receive Supplemental Security Income checks from the Federal Government at the beginning of each month. It is a regular U.S. Government check, but it is gold in color so it is easily identified when you have a question regarding payments they receive.

People 65 or older, needy people of any age who are blind or physically or mentally disabled are eligible for monthly cash payments from the U.S. Government. To qualify because of blindness a person must have central visual acuity of 20/200 or less in the better eye with corrective glasses or visual field restriction of 20 degrees or less. If an individual is unable to work and earn money due to physical or mental impairment which has lasted 12 months or longer or is expected to result in death, he is eligible for payments.

Payments can be as much as $177.80 per month for an individual and $266.70 for an eligible couple.

Payments will increase automatically with cost of living increases. Payments are smaller if applicants have other income sources.

Even though the Social Security Administration runs the program it is not Social Security. Social Security benefits are paid from the contributions of workers, employers and self-employed people, with no restrictions on amount of money and property you can have. You still get your Social Security benefits regardless of what you own or its value. Money for Supplemental Security benefits comes from U.S. Treasury general funds. If you are eligible, you can get both Social Security and Supplemental security income.

Aged, blind and disabled are eligible for Medicaid for which they may apply at their local welfare office.

Social Security. There is a great deal to know about the Social Security Administration and many ways to collect cash from the various programs offered through this program. The topic could be a book in itself; in a question and answer form the basic facts will be covered.

Question: Who is covered?

Answer: Practically everybody, if they work fairly regularly. Before 1978, you had to work a certain number of "quarters of coverage" at work covered by law. A quarter of coverage was earned if you earned $50 or more in wages in a 3 month calendar quarter. If self-employed, 4 quarters of coverage were earned. Starting in 1978, a worker received one quarter of coverage for each $250 of covered annual earnings up to a maximum of four for a year whether he was employed or self-employed.

Question: Who pays for the insurance?

Answer: Both workers and employers pay for the workers' insurance. Self-employed persons pay their own each year along with their income tax.

Question: How do I apply for benefits?

Answer: You apply for benefits by filing a claim. This can be done by mail or telephone or at any Social Security Office. The address can be obtained at any post office or in the phone book under United States Government, Department of Health, Education, and Welfare, Social Security Administration.

Question: What information will I need when I apply?

Answer: That depends on what type of benefit you are applying for. If you apply for retirement benefits, you will need a birth certificate (or baptismal). Other old documents showing proof of age such as school records, or census records may also be acceptable. If a widow is claiming benefits based on her husband's earnings, she should have proof of her age and a copy of her marriage certificate.

Question: What facts should I know about retirement benefits?

Answer: A retired worker and spouse can get full monthly benefit checks at age 65. No one ever needs credit for more than 10 years of work. Reduced payments are available as early as 62 years of age, at which time a worker can collect 80% of his full benefit.

Question: What benefits are available to aged persons in need?

Answer: Federal grants to states are authorized to pay part of the cost of financial assistance to persons 65 or over who are in need. This old-age assistance program is designed to provide aged persons (in need) with supplemental income. They may then be economically independent. This program on the state level is known as the Federal old-age insurance program. In 1956 and 1960, the Social Security Act was amended. The 1956

Amendments clarified the purpose of the Social Security Act. In 1960, additional Federal sharing in state expenditures for old-age assistance was provided. This was in the form of payments for medical care to those who provide it to the aged. Amendments in 1961 increased the amount of Federal participation in the payments to medical services.

Question: What kinds of help can I get from Social Security?

Answer: There are seven different kinds of help available to you through the Social Security Administration: 1) retirement checks, as of January 1978 workers reaching 65 may receive a $459.80 monthly benefit check, 2) disability income for people under 65 who work can receive $114.30 to $642.90 each month. Disabled people with families may receive as much as $1,125.10 each month, 3) supplemental Security Income is a separate cash program directed at the needs of people 65 years old or older or blind or disabled.

Benefits may be up to $177.80 for individuals or $266.70 for married couples, 4) survivors' benefits for the beneficiaries of a deceased worker are available to widow or widower, children, and parents, 5) medicare passed in 1965, this Amendment to the Social Security Act to aid eligible people with hospital insurance and a supplementary program covering physicians costs, 6) student benefits are available to eligible students between 18 and 22, 7) widowers' benefits are available to a man if he has not remarried and cares for an unmarried child under 18.

HOW TAX RATE WILL CHANGE

	Employees and Employer Each				Self-Employed		
	Worker's Maximum Annual Pay Taxed	Tax Rate	Maximum Tax Per Worker	Increase From Old Law	Tax Rate	Maximum Tax	Increase From Old Law
1979	$22,900	6.13%	$1,403.77	$ 260.32	8.10%	$1,854.90	$ 324.00
1980	$25,900	6.13%	$1,587.67	$ 353.47	8.10%	$2,097.90	$ 445.50
1981	$29,700	6.65%	$1,975.05	$ 595.35	9.30%	$2,762.10	$ 933.45
1982	$31,800	6.70%	$2,130.60	$ 656.40	9.35%	$2,973.30	$1,019.40
1983	$33,900	6.70%	$2,271.30	$ 702.60	9.35%	$3,169.65	$1,090.50
1984	$36,000	6.70%	$2,412.00	$ 748.80	9.35%	$3,366.00	$1,161.60
1985	$38,100	7.05%	$2,686.05	$ 928.35	9.90%	$3,771.90	$1,442.25
1986	$40,200	7.15%	$2,874.30	$ 978.00	10.0%	$4,020.00	$1,521.00
1987	$42,600	7.15%	$3,045.90	$1,033.50	10.0%	$4,260.00	$1,608.00

Special Benefits for Disabled Coal Miners ("Black Lung"). This program is designed to replace income to coal miners who have become totally disabled because of Black Lung disease or to their widows if they had been receiving benefits at the time of death or who died of the disease. In some cases where there is no widow surviving the coal miner benefits go to his children. If there are no children totally dependent parents of miners or brothers and sisters are entitled to benefits. They are also payable to the children of a widow who was receiving Black Lung benefits at the time of her death.

Monthly cash benefits are available and paid to entitled coal miners, their widows, children, parents, or brothers and sisters as the case may be. There are no restrictions on use of money received.

Becoming "totally disabled" because of Black Lung disease entitles a miner to receive benefits. He may, however, be able to work in another area (not a coal miner) and still receive benefits. If you are a widow whose husband was receiving benefits before his death, or whose husband died of Black Lung disease, you are automatically eligible to receive benefits as are children of coal miners, dependent parents, brothers and sisters should the widow receiving benefits die.

The amount of money you get is increased if there are dependents in the family. In fiscal year 1974, the average family received $253 per month and in 1975, $251 per month. An average of 463,000 miners, widows, and dependents received cash benefits under this program in fiscal year 1974. While in fiscal year 1975, it was 489,000.

For additional information contact:

> The Bureau of Disability Insurance
> Social Security Administration
> 6401 Security Blvd.
> Baltimore, Maryland 21235

EDUCATION LOANS

Department of Health, Education and Welfare

Guaranteed Loans. These are made to students enrolled in approved colleges, universities, vocational, technical or business schools. They may be used to finance post-secondary education. Applicants may apply at commercial lending institutions in their home state.

National Defense Student Loans. Funds from this source are available to students enrolled in or accepted for enrollment in participating colleges, universities or other institutions of higher learning. Low interest loans are provided to students who may apply directly to the college or university.

Cuban Refugee Loans. Cubans who became refugees after January 1, 1959, are eligible to apply for aid to continue their college education by applying directly to the college or university.

Through the Public Health Service, loans are available from the National Institute of Health for medical or nursing study.

Medical Study. Full time students enrolled or accepted for enrollment in a college or university in professional study leading to a degree in the following fields are eligible for funds. The fields include medicine, dentistry, osteopathy, optometry, pediatry, pharmacy or veterinary medicine. Students may apply to the school for financial assistance.

Nursing Study. Students enrolled or accepted for enrollment for full time study leading to a diploma, an associate degree or equivalent degree, baccalaureate or an advanced degree in nursing may apply for assistance to the school.

Regional Offices Health, Education and Welfare Department

Region I	Address/Telephone
Massachusetts, New Hampshire, Maine, Rhode Island, Vermont, Connecticut	John F. Kennedy Federal Bldg. Boston, Massachusetts 02203 (617) 223-6831

Region II

New York, New Jersey	26 Federal Plaza New York, New York 10007 (212) 264-4600

Region III

Pennsylvania, Virginia, Washington, D.C., Maryland, West Virginia, Delaware	3535 Market St. Philadelphia, Pennsylvania 19101 (215) 597-1114

Region IV

Kentucky, Alabama, Florida, South Carolina, North Carolina, Mississippi, Tennessee, Georgia	50-7th St. N.E. Atlanta, Georgia 30323 (404) 526-5817

Regional Offices Health, Education and Welfare Dept. (cont.)

Region V	Address/Telephone
Michigan, Ohio, Wisconsin, Minnesota, Illinois, Indiana	300 South Wacker Dr. Chicago, Illinois 60606 (312) 353-5160

Region VI

Louisiana, Arkansas, Texas, Oklahoma, New Mexico	1114 Commerce St. Dallas, Texas 75202 (214) 749-3396

Region VII

Kansas, Missouri, Nebraska, Iowa	601 East 12th St. Kansas City, Missouri 64106 (816) 374-3436

Region VIII

Colorado, Montana, North Dakota, South Dakota, Utah, Wyoming	1961 Stout St. Denver, Colorado 80202 (303) 837-3373

Region IX

California, Hawaii, Nevada, Arizona	50 Fulton St. San Francisco, California 94102 (415) 556-6746

Region X

Oregon, Washington,
Idaho, Alaska

1321 2nd Ave.
Seattle, Washington 98101
(206) 442-0420

CHAPTER II

U.S. DEPARTMENT OF AGRICULTURE

WHAT IS THE DEPARTMENT OF AGRICULTURE?

This department was established on May 15, 1862 as a commission and in 1889 was made an executive department. Its purpose is to promote the general interests of those who produce from the soil. This includes ranchers, farmers, homesteaders, tenants or private corporations. Rural communities are assisted in conserving and improving land, water and forestry as well as home management; so they may eliminate problems like malnutrition.

The various agencies of the U.S. Department of Agriculture have specific functions. For instance, the Agricultural Stabilization and Conservation Service deals with price support and production-adjustment programs. These programs are financed by Commodity Credit Corporation. These and other agencies and their functions are listed in the following chart.

UNITED STATES DEPARTMENT OF AGRICULTURE

Agency	Function
The Agricultural Stabilization and Conservation Service (ASCS)	price-support and production-adjustment programs
The Commodity Credit Corporation	finances the programs of the ASCS
The Federal Crop Insurance Corporation	insures crop-production costs against loss from weather, insects and diseases
The Farmer Cooperative Service	helps farmers with self-help programs
The Foreign Agricultural Service	market development (expands exports)

The Farmers Home Administration	extends credit to farmers, finances rural housing, water and sewage systems, small rural business enterprises
The Rural Electrification Administration	bring electric and telephone service to rural people
The Soil Conservation Service	provides technical and financial help to individuals and communities in conserving and improving land and water resources, classifies soil in a nation wide system.
The Forest Service	manages the countries 155 national forests and 19 national grasslands
The Agricultural Research Service	work closely with state agricultural stations and forestry institutions in

Cooperative State Research Service	doing research. This research is on production marketing and usage of agricultural products, control and eradication of plant and animal diseases, as well as, nutritional research
The Economic Research Service	provide economic and statistical information on crops and livestock, prices and income, rural development and conservation and foreign agriculture and other data
The Statistical Reporting Service	
The Extension Service	through education, they help farmers, rural residents and general public apply research and technology
The Agricultural Marketing Service	grades and inspects agricultural com-

	modities, provides marketing services
The Food and Nutrition Service	administers food stamps program and other programs of food assistance

HOW CAN I GET MONEY FROM THE U.S. DEPARTMENT OF AGRICULTURE

There are many ways an eligible person can get cash from the government through the Department of Agriculture. Loans, insured by private lenders or guaranteed by the government are available to those who qualify.

The county or area committee of the Farmers Home Administration determines eligibility for the funds discussed in this section. In most cases the applicant must have farm background and experience or training necessary to be successful in the proposed operation. They must be of good character and possess the ability and industry to carry out the proposed farming operation or operation of proposed recreational facility. The applicant must be able to manage and operate the farm and be a citizen of legal age. He must also be unable to get credit from another source at reasonable rates and terms to finance his needs. After the loan is made he must be an owner or tenant operating not larger than a family farm.

If you want to do any of the following things and meet the eligibility requirements the government has money for you!

    Purchase and develop farms

    Build and improve rural homes and essential farm buildings

    Provide rental housing for senior citizens

    Develop water supplies and carry out soil conservation measures

    Build housing for farm laborers

    Develop watersheds

    Cover damage costs from natural disaster such as flood or drought

    Repair your home

    Buy land to build your home on

    Buy a house

    and countless other reasons

Read through each portion of this book carefully to determine which program suits your needs best. If for some reason you have difficulty refer to the directory and consult your regional or local agency. They will be glad to assist you.

The Food and Nutrition Service is another agency of the U.S. Department of Agriculture that has money for you. It administers the food stamp program and other food assistance programs to children and the needy. In this way low-income families and those receiving public assistance can buy more and better quality food.

Those meeting national eligibility requirements are issued an identification card to prove their eligibility. The amount of benefit received varies with the size of family and net monthly income.

If you are a low-income family or a large family without sufficient means of feeding your family adequately this program is well worth looking into. Read the section of this book that discusses the food stamp program and the programs of food distribution. You'll find a list of eligibility requirements and benefits available. It will tell you exactly how to get what you need or sources of information who can assist you.

The Department of Agriculture offers many programs of assistance. You owe it to yourself to find out what money you can receive from them. There are numerous programs available. We discuss many of them in this book, but there are even more! We can tell you how to get the money and from which source, but it's up to you to follow through.

If these programs discussed don't fit your needs exactly, contact the sources mentioned and they can assist you.

WHAT IS THE FARMER'S HOME ADMINISTRATION?

The Farmer's Home Administration makes most of the loans to farmers who carry on farming operations on a scale large enough to support their family. Each loan is based on a plan designed to provide enough income from the farm and other sources so the family may enjoy a standard of living that is reasonable and be able to pay their debts when they are due.

Supervisors in each county help the farmers with farm, home, and management problems. Where adjustments and improvements are major, the Farmer's Home

Administration supervisors meet the borrowers at the end of each year to help them discover strong and weak points in their farming operations. They assist in developing plans for further improvements within the coming year.

Veterans with farm experience who apply receive preference.

Local county offices of the Farmer's Home Administration are usually localed in countyseat towns. All applications for loans are made in these offices. Eligibility of each applicant is certified by a county or area committee of three farmers. They also have the ability and power to decide the maximum amount of each loan and to review the progress of the borrower.

The loans granted under this program supplement, but are not to compete with, credit available from other lenders.

There are several ways in which the Farmer's Home Administration serves the credit needs of farmers who cannot obtain funds from other sources. First of all, they supply technical farm and financial management assistance along with each loan. They also advance credit based on ability of the farmer to repay. This safeguard works for the agency, as well as the farmer because he will not owe more than he can afford to pay. Finally, the loan amounts may not exceed the appraised value of the security.

In some cases, though they may not be eligible for a Farmers Home Administration loan, they will be provided with assistance in determining, credit needs, debt repayment schedules and solutions to other problems of financial management.

Loans are made from funds provided by Congress or on an insured basis from funds provided by private lenders.

Full explanation about loans and services available may be obtained from supervisors at local county Farmers Home Administration. If you are unable to locate your local office write or call:

U.S. Department of Agriculture
Farmers Home Administration
14th and Independence S.W.
Washington, D.C. 20250
(202) 447-2791

The addresses and phone numbers of the regional offices of the U.S. Department of Agriculture are included in a directory in this book, following the detailed description of loans and funds available to farmers.

HOW I CAN GET MONEY FROM THE FARMERS HOME ADMINISTRATION?

Farmers Home Administration offers credit and technical help needed on a farm or for money management problems.

Operating Loans. These loans are made to eligible farm operators so they may make better use of land and labor. Funds may be used to pay for (1) Feed (2) Seed (3) Livestock (4) Equipment (5) Fertilizer (6) Other farm and home operating needs (7) Refinancing chattel debts (8) Operating credit to fish farmers (9) Carrying out forestry purposes (10) Developing income - producing recreational enterprises.

Loans are scheduled to be repaid in accordance with the ability of the borrower to repay. However, the time is not to exceed 7 years.

In order to be eligible you must (1) have the farm experience, background or training necessary to be successful in the operation (2) be a U.S. citizen of legal age (3) be unable to obtain sufficient credit elsewhere on reasonable terms (4) have the ability and character to carry out the proposed operation (5) not conduct a larger than family farming operation as tenant or owner after making the loan (6) be not more than 21 years of age and live in a rural town or area of not more than 10,000 in order to receive loans for project financing for 4-H, Future Farmers, Future Homemakers or similar organizations.

In 1973 fiscal year, for example, loans totaling approximately four hundred fifty four million dollars were made. The average loan was $8,900. They ranged from $100 to $50,000. 51,000 such loans were granted in 1973. At the present time over all, approximately 77,000 are still outstanding. For additional information write to:

U.S. Department of Agriculture
Farmers Home Administration
14th and Independence S.W.
Washington, D.C. 20250
(202) 447-2791

Farm ownership loans are offered to assist eligible farmers or ranchers by extending credit and supervisory

42

assistance so they may (1) make efficient use of their land and other resources (2) carry on successful operations on the farm (3) be given the opportunity to maintain a reasonable standard of living.

These loans are made to eligible farmers so they may (1) enlarge, develop or buy farms (not larger than family size) (2) refinance debts (3) provide real estate credit to fish farmers (4) carry out forestry purposes (5) develop income producing recreational enterprises.

Each loan is scheduled to be repaid according to the borrower's ability to repay but the time period may not exceed 40 years.

In order to be eligible the applicant must (1) be unable to obain necessary and sufficient credit at reasonable terms from any other source (2) be a U.S. citizen of legal age (3) have training experience and ability to run a family farm or non farm enterprise (4) be of good character (5) be agreeable to refinance when sufficient credit on reasonable terms is available from another source.

The loans average around $28,000, and vary considerably in size depending upon the needs of applicants. The amounts range from $18,800 to $100,000.

In fiscal year 1973 about 15, 400 loans were granted. For more information on farm ownership loans you may write to:

U.S. Department of Agriculture
Farmers Home Administration
14th and Independence S.W.
Washington, D.C. 20250
(202) 447-2791

Irrigation, Drainage and Other Soil Conservation Loans are offered to (1) increase the income of farm families and other rural residents and (2) to readjust the use of land in order to better serve the community.

Loans for development, use and conservation of water and land are made to eligible individuals and groups of farmers and rural residents so they may (1) develop systems of water supply for irrigation, livestock or household use (2) drain farm land (3) carry out soil conservation.

Each loan is scheduled for repayment according to borrower's ability to repay. It may not exceed 40 years, depending on the type of loan the interest rate varies.

Non-profit public bodies and corporations which serve residents of rural areas or towns and villages of up to

5,500 population may receive assistance when (1) they cannot get adequate funds at reasonable rates from other sources (2) the improvements will serve farmers and rural residents and (3) they have the ability legally to borrow, repay and offer security for the loan and operate the facility or service.

Loans to individuals average approximately $5,000 and to associations $100,000.

Sizes of loans vary considerably depending on the applicants needs. In individual loan cases, total indebtedness of the individual on the farm may not be more than $60,000 or the securities normal value (whichever is less). If the loan is to a group or association, their total indebtedness may not exceed $500,000.

For more information get in contact with:

U.S. Department of Agriculture
Farmers Home Administration
14th and Independence S.W.
Washington, D.C. 20250
(202) 447-7967

Rural Home Site Loans are available to public or private nonprofit organizations interested in providing sites for housing, so they may buy and develop land in rural areas. This land may be subdivided as building sites and sold on a nonprofit basis. It may be sold to low and moderate income families, cooperatives and nonprofit applicants.

Uses of funds include (1) purchase and development of sites and equipment which becomes a permanent part of the development such as water and sewer facilities (2) payment of closing costs, legal fees or engineering (3) landscaping and related things such as sidewalks, parking areas or driveways. Limitations include certain restrictions on uses. They may not be used for refinancing of debts or paying fees or commission to brokers or such persons, for referral of applicants or solicitation of loan funds. Funds may not be used to pay operating costs or administration expenses other than actual cash cost of incidental administrative expenses if funds are not available from other sources.

These loans vary greatly with type and use. Direct loans average about $9,000 while insured loans range from $58,700 to $570,000. The average insured loan is $376,225. During 1973 for example, 20 insured and one direct loan were made. In fiscal year 1974 estimates show one direct and seven insured loans were granted. The

1975 fiscal year estimate is one direct and nine insured loans.

During each of the fiscal years on an average of at least 1,000 sites were provided.

Both applicants and their beneficiaries may be eligible. Applicants must be a public or private nonprofit organization that will provide the developed sites to qualified borrowers on a nonprofit basis. Beneficiary eligibility includes (1) Families that are eligible for low and moderate-income. Section 502 Rural Housing Loans including self-help housing (2) Nonprofit rural rental housing applicants also (3) Applicants eligible for HUD Section 235 and 236 insured mortgages. For additional information:

U.S. Department of Agriculture
Farmers Home Administration
14th and Independence S.W.
Washington, D.C. 20250
(202) 447-5177

Recreation Facility Loans are granted to assist farm and ranch owners and tenants to convert all or part of their farms to income-producing outdoor recreational facilities. This income, to aid the farmer in carrying on a successful and sound enterprise, therefore supplementing the farm or ranch income. Besides the extension of credit, farmers and ranchers are offered supervisory assistance.

Funds may be used for (1) the development of water and land resources (2) construction of buildings (3) repair of buildings (4) purchase of land, equipment, livestock and related recreation items (5) payment of operating expenses, campgrounds, stables (at horseback riding facilities), swimming facilities, tennis courts, shooting preserves, vacation cottages, lakes, ponds (for boating and fishing), lodges and rooms for visitors, docks, nature trails, hunting preserves, and areas for skiing and other winter sports are some recreational enterprises that might be financed.

Types of assistance are both insured loans and guaranteed loans.

To be eligible for assistance an applicant must (1) not be able to get credit needed at reasonable terms (2) be a citizen of the United States of legal age (3) be agreeable to refinancing the balance due of his loan at the earliest time that credit needed is available at reasonable terms from another credit source (4) be engaged in farming when the loan is made (5) have the training and/or experience

48

needed to be successful in the proposed enterprise.

Other related programs include Resource Conservation and Development Loans and Outdoor Recreation Technical Assistance.

Loans range in amount from $6,500 to $100,000, depending on need and eligibility of the applicant.

Very Low-Income Housing Repair Loans are offered to eligible very low-income rural homeowners so they may maintain safe homes free from health hazards. These loans give them the funds with which to make minor repairs. Both guaranteed and insured loans are available.

Uses and restrictions on Very Low-Income Housing Repair Loans assist owner-occupants in rural areas who do not qualify for Section 502 loans to repair or improve their homes. In this way, they can make their homes safe and clean and free of health hazards. The repairs may include fixing roof, foundation or basic structure, as well as the water or sewage system. $2,500 is the maximum amount of a loan for the improvement of any one farm or non-farm. If the improvement involves bathroom or kitchen with water and waste disposal system or plumbing supplies, loans will not be made for the construction of new homes under this program.

In order to be eligible an applicant must 1) own and live on a farm or rural non-farm tract, 2) not be able to qualify for a Section 502 loan, and 3) be able to repay the loan.

These loans range from $300 to $3,500. In 1974 approximately 2,500 loans were granted totalling about 3 million dollars.

For assistance or further information call or write:

U.S. Department of Agriculture
Farmers Home Administration
14th and Independence S.W.
Washington, D.C. 20250
(202) 447-5177

Rural Rental Housing Loans are available to provide rental or cooperative housing for rural residents. This is housing that is economically designed and constructed.

Both guaranteed and insured loans are available under this particular program.

Funds acquired under this loan program can be used to 1) construct, 2) purchase, 3) improve, or 4) repair rental or cooperative housing, 5) provide recreational and service type facilities used in connection with housing, 6) buy land on which buildings are to be constructed. The housing may be duplex units, apartment buildings or individual single family housing. Loans may not be made for nursing, special care, or institutional-type homes.

Loans range in amount. Those granted to individuals vary from $17,000 to $750,000. Loans to organizations range between $43,400 to $750,000.

In order to be eligible applicants must be unable to obtain credit from another source or be unable to finance the housing themselves. Applicants may be non-profit organizations, corporate individuals or cooperatives. They must be able to furnish adequate security, have income sufficient to repay the loan and intend and be capable of maintaining and operating the housing for which the loan was made. Beneficiary eligibility include occupants who are low to moderate-income families or senior citizens.

For additional information:

> U.S. Department of Agriculture
> Farmers Home Administration
> 14th and Independence S.W.
> Washington, D.C. 20250
> (202) 447-5177

Rural Self-Help Housing Technical Assistance. Project grants are available through this program to provide financial support (money) to promote the availability of technical and supervisory assistance to help needy low-income people and their families to help themselves.

Various organizations use the money from this program 1) to hire people to carry out a technical assistance program for self-help housing in rural areas, 2) to pay office expenses, 3) to make power tools and equipment available to families who want to build their own home, 4) to pay for training self-help group members in building techniques, 5) for professional services needed. Money cannot be used to pay people for construction work, or to buy real estate, building materials or to pay any debts, expenses or costs other than those outlined in the self-help projects.

In 1974 fiscal year, $4,572,580 in loan funds were received. Loans range from $1,400 to $100,000.

To be eligible the applicant must be 1) unable to get credit from any other source at reasonable terms, 2) of legal age, 3) of good character, 4) have the training, ability, and experience to carry out the operation intended.

For more detailed information:

U.S. Department of Agriculture
Farmers Home Administration
14th and Independence S.W.
Washington, D.C. 20250
(202) 447-5177

Water Bank Program. Advisory services and counseling as well as project grants are available through the Water Bank Program to conserve surface waters, preserve and improve waterfowl and wildlife resources.

For 10 years eligible landowners agree to help preserve important breeding and nesting areas of migratory waterfowl. This may be renewed for additional periods of time. During the time of the agreement these landowners agree not to drain, burn, fill or destroy, in any way, the natural habitat of the area, or to use the area for agricultural purposes (as determined by the Secretary of the U.S. Department of Agriculture). The secretary, will, in turn, carry out the program in harmony with wetlands programs administered by the Secretary of the Interior and use whatever technical and related services of the State, Federal and private conservation agencies to assure this harmony.

Those eligible include: landowners and operators of specified types of wetlands in areas specified for migratory waterfowl nesting and breeding.

In the fiscal year 1973, 90,000 acres were placed under agreements.

For additional information consult:

Environmental Quality and Land Use Division
Agricultural Stabilization and
    Conservation Service
U.S. Department of Agriculture
Washington, D.C. 20250
(202) 447-7967

Rural Environmental Conservation Program. Through cost sharing, this program helps farmers, ranchers and woodland owners carry out approved soil, water, woodland, forestry incentives and wildlife. The wildlife conservation practices must also conserve soil and water. Those involved in the program are responsible for the upkeep and maintenance of practices established with cost-share assistance.

Those eligible must bear part of the cost of an approved conservation practice. This includes owners, landlords, tenants or sharecroppers on a farm or ranch; also associated groups.

The amount of assistance varies from $3 to $2,500 for individuals and $3 to $10,000 for groups.

For additional information consult the headquarters office:

> Agricultural Stabilization and
>   Conservation Service
> U.S. Department of Agriculture
> Washington, D.C. 20250
> (202) 447-7967

Rural Housing Loans are made for the construction and repair of homes and essential farm buildings so eligible farmers and owners of non-farm land in rural areas may obtain safe, adequate housing and other related facilities.

Funds may be used (1) to repair, construct or purchase housing (2) obtain adequate disposal facilities for sewage necessary for the applicant and his family (3) buy land on which the applicant wishes to build a home or place a dwelling (i.e. house trailer) (4) to purchase or install equipment which becomes part of the real estate once installed.

There are some restrictions on the use of loans and they include: size, design and cost of a financed dwelling for a low or moderate income family must be modest. In addition, the applicant must be unable to provide the necessary housing and/or essential farm buildings or related facilities on his own account and be unable to obtain credit needed from other sources at reasonable terms.

Insured loans may be granted for the financing of housing facilities for domestic farm labor to individual farmers, groups of farmers and public or private nonprofit organizations.

Housing loans to people in rural areas who are 62 years of age or older may be granted so they may build homes, improve their own homes or buy previously owned and occupied housing. They can also use funds to purchase a dwelling site. If their ability to repay does not meet requirements they may use co-signers.

Repayment of loans is scheduled according to the borrower's ability to pay. The period may not exceed 33 years.

Those eligible must (1) be, or become at the closing of the loan, owners of a farm or nonfarm tract in a rural area. (2) be a citizen of the U.S. or reside in the U.S. after being legally admitted for permament residence. (3) have income available and adequate for operating and living expenses (including taxes, insurance, and maintenance) and repayment of proposed loan and other debts.

In certain cases lower income families may be granted lower interest rates depending on the size and income of the applicant family.

These loans average $15,500 and vary considerably in size from $9,000 to $22,000 depending upon the needs of the individual applicant.

For additional information write to:

U.S. Dept. of Agriculture
Farmers Home Administration
14th and Independence S.W.
Washington, D.C. 20250
(202) 447-5177

Emergency Loans are granted to farmers when credit from other sources is not available in areas where a natural disaster such as a flood or drought has occured and the farmer needs temporary help.

Loans may be made for the purchase of feed, seed,

fertilizer, replacement of equipment or livestock, any other related items needed to continue operations. They may not be used for refinancing debts or compensation for losses. Oyster planters and ranchers may receive loans if eligible. Loans many also be used to cover real estate repairs needed because of the disaster. In cases of damaged or destroyed crops, the loan is made to cover the cost of the crops up till the time they were destroyed.

The amount of the loan may not be more than the amount of the loss suffered and must be within the applicants ability to repay.

When losses are physical the loan amount will be based on the cost of repairing, restoring or replacing farm property that was damaged. This may include home furnishings and personal possessions. Some loans may include funds to cover production expenses.

Applicants are required to produce itemized statements of expenditures for which they seek reimbursement.

In order to receive assistance, a county must be named by the Federal Disaster Assistance Administration as eligible under a Presidential declaration of a major disaster or be designated as an emergency loan area by the Secretary of Agriculture or authorized by the State Director of the Farm Housing Administration when not more than 25 farmers or ranchers in a county have been affected by the disaster.

The repayment of loans is scheduled when the income from the crop or livestock financed is normally received.

To be eligible you must (1) be an established farmer or rancher (2) be a United States citizen (3) suffer severe loss of crops, livestock, or property damage caused by a natural disaster and not covered by insurance or other compensation.

The average loan is $7,000. They vary considerably in size depending on the actual needs of the applicant and the system of farming to be financed. Loans range from 3,000 to 50,000 dollars.

For additional information write to:

> U.S. Dept. of Agriculture
> Farmers Home Administration
> 14th and Independence S.W.
> Washington, D.C. 20250
> (202) 447-2791

Watershed Loans are made to protect and develop land and water resources in small watersheds. Local organizations may be granted a loan to help finance projects with the same objective.

Loans may be used to help local organizations provide the local share of the cost of improvements for flood prevention, irrigation, drainage, water quality management, sedimentation control, development of fish and wildlife, public water based recreation and water storage.

Repayment schedules vary and may be up to 50 years.

Eligible local organizations include irrigation districts, conservation districts, drainage districts, flood control and prevention districts, soil and conservation districts, municipal corporations, non-profit irrigation or reservoir companies, mutual water companies, water user's associations and similar organizations.

In addition, the applicant must have the authority under the state law to obtain, give security for and raise funds to repay the loan and to operate and maintain the facility to be financed with the loan.

The average loan is $227,000. Loans range from $7,000 to $2,000,000. A loan outstanding in any one watershed cannot exceed $5,000,000.

For more information write:

U.S. Department of Agriculture
Farmers Home Administration
14th and Independence S.W.
Washington, D.C. 20250
(202) 447-2791

WHAT IS THE FOOD AND NUTRITION SERVICE?

The Food and Nutrition Service is an agency of the U.S. Department of Agriculture. Through food distribution programs your children can receive hot well-balanced lunches at school. The Food Stamp program is also operated by the U.S.D.A. to assist low income families to purchase more and better quality food. This agency provides food to those aged, in need of assistance through formula grants, sale, and exchange or donation of goods.

HOW CAN I GET MONEY FROM THE FOOD AND NUTRITION SERVICE?

Direct payments are available in the form of coupons with which those eligible may purchase food. The amount varies with amount of net income and size of family. Recently new laws were passed with regard to manner in which the benefits are made available. Up until now people eligible bought food stamps. For example, for $20.00 you could purchase food coupons worth $38.00 thereby getting $38.00 worth of food for $20.00. Now eligible individuals have an I.D. card. They show the card and get the amount of coupons to which they are entitled according to their income and circumstance.

Contact your local welfare department for more information. They are listed in the telephone directory under U.S. Government.

DEPARTMENT OF AGRICULTURE

Food and Nutrition Service. Food stamps and distribution of food stuffs.

Households determined to be in need of food assistance by public welfare agencies are issued I.D. cards enabling them to receive assistance to supplement their food purchasing power. In this way, low income families are able to buy more and better quality food than they can ordinarily afford. Food coupons may not be used for certain items. These include cocoa, coffee, tea, bananas, alcoholic beverages, tobacco or any product which is clearly identified on the package as being imported from foreign sources.

Food distribution programs help improve the diets of needy persons and school children. Under their programs food is made available for distribution to individuals, schools, the elderly, charitable institutions, summer camps, and qualifying households. Food that is donated is not for sale. It may not be sold, exchanged, or otherwise disposed of with Department approval.

Formula grants to aid in administering food distribution for needy persons in households are available through this program. These funds may not be used for purchasing property.

For more information on the food stamps program contact: Director, Food Stamp Division
Food and Nutrition Service
U.S. Department of Agriculture
Washington, D.C. 20250
(202) 447-8982

For more information on the food distribution program, call or write to:
Food Distribution Division
Food and Nutrition Service
U.S. Department of Agriculture
Washington, D.C. 20250
(202) 447-8371

RURAL ELECTRIFICATION ADMINISTRATION

Type	Use	Applicants	Where To Apply
Power and Telephone Facilities	Build and operate power plants to supply service in rural areas; improve telephone lines; finance purchase of wiring, plumbing, and electric equipment or appliances	Telephone companies and non-profit cooperatives and mutual associations Nonprofit cooperatives, power districts, and other public agencies, and electric companies	Rural Electrification Administration, U.S. Department of Agriculture, Washington, D.C. 20250.

COMMODITY CREDIT CORPORATION

Type	Use	Applicants	Where To Apply
Agricultural	Loans on commodities stored on farms or in warehouses	Farmers	Agrigultural Stabilization & Conservation Service local office.
	To build or enlarge storage areas or drying equipment	Farmers	Agrigultural Stabilization & Conservation Service local office.

FARMERS CREDIT ADMINISTRATION

Type	Use	Applicants	Where To Apply
Bank Loans For Cooperatives	Loan service for farmer cooperatives	Farmers Cooperatives	Bank for Cooperatives
Federal land Bank	Long-term mortgage credit to buy, expand, improve farms or refinance debts	Farmers and farming corporations	Federal land bank associations
Production Credit Associations	short and intermediate term credit	Farmers and farming corporations	Production credit association
Adminis-trating	Improve land, labor, equipment; develop resources including non-farm and recreational enterprises	Farmers	Farmers Home Administration Office

FARMERS HOME ADMINISTRATION

Type	Use	Applicants	Where to Apply
Farm Ownership	To buy or improve farms and to provide buildings and land for non-farm enterprises needed to supplement farm incomes	Farmers and ranchers of not larger than family farms	Local FHA Office

Type	Use	Applicants	Where To Apply
Conservation	Develop, conserve, and improve use of soil and water resources	Individual farm operators and owners, partnerships and domestic corporations engaged in farming	Local FHA Office
Resource Conservation and Development	To improve the economy in areas designated as Resource Conservation and Development Project areas by the Secretary of Agriculture	Public bodies, and nonprofit corporations	Local FHA Office in area
Comprehensive Area Plans	Grants for water and sewer systems in rural areas	Public bodies, State, regional, local planning commissions	Local FHA Office
Labor Housing Grants	Domestic farm labor housing	Public bodies or broadly-based nonprofit organizations	Local FHA Office
Self-Help Housing	To build houses for individuals under supervision of a construction expert	Groups of low income rural families or low income urban families employed in a rural area	Local FHA Office

Type	Use	Applicants	Where To Apply
Technical Assistance Self-Help Housing	Technical assistance for self-help housing	Public bodies or private nonprofit corporations	Local FHA Office
Rural Housing Site Loans	To buy land to be used for building low and moderate families' homes	Public or private nonprofit corporations	Local FHA Office
Conditional Commitments	To assure builder or seller that homes will meet FHA lending requirements if built as proposed and that the agency would be willing to make loans to qualified applicants who may want to buy homes	Individual, partnership or corporations engaged in construction of homes	Local FHA Office
Disaster	Where natural disasters (flood and droughts) have brought about a need for credit not available from other sources temporarily	Farmers	Local FHA Office
Watershed	Finance projects that protect and develop land and water resources in small watersheds	Local organizations	Local FHA Office

Type	Use	Applicants	Where To Apply
Economic Opportunity	Loans to low income families in rural areas to help them to increase their incomes; also, to cooperatives serving low income rural people and providing processing, purchasing, or marketing services	Low income rural families	Local FHA Office
*Water and waste disposal programs	Construction of community water and waste disposal systems in rural areas	Public bodies and nonprofit organizations	Local FHA Office
*Recreation	Construction of rural outdoor recreation facilities	Public bodies and nonprofit organizations	Local FHA Office
Irrigation	Develop irrigation systems, drain farmland, and carry out soil conservation measures	Groups of farmers and ranchers	Local FHA Office
Grazing and Forest Lands	Loans to develop grazing area and forest lands	Groups of farmers and ranchers	Local FHA Office

*Agency authorized to make recreation loans to commmunity groups, but funds limited and program has been assigned secondary priority to farm operation, housing, and water and sewer.

Type	Use	Applicants	Where To Apply
Rural Housing	To build and repair home and essential farm buildings, purchase previously occupied homes or buy sites on which to build homes	Farmers and other residents in open country and rural communities of not more than 5,500	Local FHA Office
Rural Rental Housing	Loans to provide rental housing for the elderly and younger residents of low and moderate income in rural areas	Individuals, profit corporations, private non-profit corporations	Local FHA Office
Cooperative Housing	Develop cooperative housing for the elderly and younger residents of low and moderate income in rural areas	Consumer cooperatives, housing cooporatives and non-profit corporations that can legally operate a housing cooperative	Local FHA Office

Type	Use	Applicants	Where To Apply
Housing For Labor	Loans to finance housing facilities for domestic farm labor	Individual farmers, groups of farmers, and public or private non-profit organizations	Local FHA Office

Regional Offices Agriculture Department

Region I	Address/Telephone
Massachusetts, New Hampshire, Maine, Rhode Island, Vermont, Connecticut	141 Milk St. Boston, Massachusetts 02109 (617) 223-5261

Region II	
New York, New Jersey	26 Federal Plaza New York, New York 10007 (212) 264-8024

Region III	
Pennsylvania, Virginia, Washington, D.C., Maryland, West Virginia, Delaware	3535 Market St. Philadelphia, Pennsylvania 19102 (215) 597-1114

70

Region IV	*Address/Telephone*
Kentucky, Alabama, Florida, South Carolina, North Carolina, Mississippi, Tennessee, Georgia	Closed-Atlanta, Georgia
Region VI	
Louisiana, Arkansas, Texas, Oklahoma, New Mexico	Brian and Ervay Sts. Dallas, Texas 75221 (214) 749-7281
Region VII	
Colorado, Montana, North Dakota, South Dakota, Utah, Wyoming	6740 East Hampden Ave. Denver, Colorado 80222 (303) 837-4248
Region IX	
California, Hawaii, Nevada, Arizona	120 Montgomery St. San Francisco, California 94104 (415) 556-5696

Region X	*Address/Telephone*
Oregon, Washington, Idaho, Alaska	1816 Federal Bldg. Seattle, Washington 98174 (206) 442-5742
At Large	Federal Center Bldg. 710 Denver, Colorado 80225 (303) 234-2469

District Offices Farm Credit Administration - Federal Land Banks

District I	*Address/Telephone*
Connecticut, Maine, Massachusetts, New Hampshire, New Jersey, New York, Rhode Island, Vermont	Box 141 Springfield, Massachusetts 01101 (413) 737-1481
District II	
Delaware, Washington, D.C., Maryland, Pennsylvania, Virginia, West Virginia	P.O. Box 1555 Baltimore, Maryland 21203 (301) 235-9100

District III	Address/Telephone
Florida, Georgia, North Carolina, South Carolina	Box 1499 Columbia, South Carolina 29202 (803) 253-3361
District IV	
Indiana, Kentucky, Ohio, Tennessee	P.O. Box 239 Louisville, Kentucky 40201 (502) 582-2621
District V	
Alabama, Louisana, Mississippi	Box 50590 New Orleans, Louisiana 70150 (504) 586-8101
District VI	
Arkansas, Illinois, Missouri	Main Post Office Box 491 St. Louis, Missouri 63166 (314) 342-3380
District VII	
Michigan, Minnesota, North Dakota, Wisconsin	375 Jackson St. St. Paul, Minnesota 55101 (612) 725-7701

73

District VIII	Address/Telephone
Iowa, Nebraska, South Dakota, Wyoming	Box 1242 Omaha, Nebraska 68101 (402) 341-2904
District IX	
Colorado, Kansas, New Mexico, Oklahoma	900 Farm Credit Banks Building 151 N. Main St. Wichita, Kansas 67202

CHAPTER III

U.S. DEPARTMENT OF THE TREASURY

WHAT IS THE TREASURY DEPARTMENT?

This department of the government maintains two primary responsibilities. The Secretary of the Treasury serves as fiscal advisor to the President and the department administers most revenue collections, the manufacture of coin and currency and many law enforcement activities.

The main divisions of work in the Treasury are; The Fiscal Service, Bureau of the Mint, Bureau of Engraving and Printing, U.S. Savings Bonds Division, Office of the Comptroller of Currency, Internal Revenue Service, Bureau of Customs, and the U.S. Secret Service.

HOW CAN I GET MONEY FROM THE
U.S. TREASURY DEPARTMENT

There are several means of collecting money from the U.S. Government through the Treasury Department. Individuals occasionally over pay income tax. The Internal Revenue Service refunds an average of $395.00 to the average American. Another way of collecting money is to turn in people whom you know are cheating on their taxes. It's call an Informant's Claim. What some people call "The Negative Income Tax" is still another means of getting money from the Treasury Department.

HOW CAN I GET MONEY FROM THE IRS?

Refunds on income tax. About 66 million Americans receive tax refunds on the taxes they pay. The average is about $395.00. By writing your local Internal Revenue Service office and asking for Refund form 1040 A you can find out if you are entitled to a refund. Fill out the form. You may even request their free pamphlet which tells you if you are entitled to a refund and how to apply. Mail the completed form back and they will notify you.

Informant's Claim. Did you know the Federal government will pay you to turn in people who are cheating on their federal income tax?

The Internal Revenue Service Code in section 7623 under the heading "Rewards for Information Relating to Violations of Internal Revenue Laws" makes you eligible. You may collect up to 10% of the "take." The information you provide must lead to the detection and punishment of the person guilty of violating the law.

All you have to do is write a letter, call or visit the I.R.S. Director of Intelligence. If they feel your "tip" is reliable information the audit division is notified. You will have to fill out Form 211 with the Informant's Claim division.

"Negative Income Tax". In 1975 a tax reduction law was passed under which the Internal Revenue Service will pay a rebate to some low income persons. To be eligible you must earn an income on which the tax is less than an earned income credit and support a child.

This means that even if your income for the year was so low that you didn't have to file a tax return you may be entitled to a refund, even if you have no refund due to witholding, you should check into this. It can be as much as $400.00.

No one with an adjusted gross income of $8,000.00 or more can be eligible. The government sends you money

77

instead of you sending them money with your income tax return, so many people refer to this as "Negative Income Tax."

Your nearest Internal Revenue Service Office can supply additional information and send you the proper form. (1040 or 1040 A)

If you earned $8,000.00 or less check with them immediately. They are listed in your local telephone directory under U.S. Government.

CHAPTER IV

U.S. DEPARTMENT OF LABOR

WHAT IS THE U.S. DEPARTMENT OF LABOR?

The Labor Department promotes the welfare of wage earners in the United States. In 1884 the Bureau of Labor was created under the Department of the Interior. On March 4, 1913 it became the U.S. Department of Labor. Besides the wage earners welfare, this deppartment seeks to improve their working conditions and increase empployment opportunities. Some of the assistance received by the Department of Labor is in the form of training and other empployment services. Some is in the form of direct money benefits.

HOW CAN I GET MONEY FROM THE U.S. DEPPARTMENT OF LABOR?

If you've had an accident on the job it administers accident-compensation. If you are a veteran they can assist you in obtaining employment. Coal miners with black lung can receive money. Longshorement and harbor workers are eligible for benefits.

The addresses and phone numbers of the regional office of the Labor Department are in the directory following this section.

U.S. DEPARTMENT OF LABOR

Longshoremen's and Harbor Worker's Compensation provides money for disability or death resulting from injury (including occupational disease to eligible private employees). Both income repplacement and supplement are provided. There are cash benefits for those who have suffered loss of sight or hearing, dismemberment or disfigurement. This includes ppayment of medical expenses (including hospital care) and funeral expenses up to $1,000. Benefits are paid by private insurance carriers of self-insured employers. In certain cases, such as permanent disability or for rehabilitation or in cases of second injury, Federal payments are available.

To be eligible you must be, 1) a longshoreman, 2) a harbor worker, 3) employed on navigational waters of the U.S. and adjoining piers and dock areas, 4) engaged in activities on the Outer Continental Shelf, 5) an employee engaged in work outside the U.S. under contract with the United States government, 6) and others specified, including survivors of the above. Under an extension of the act, employees of pprivate concerns in the District of Columbia and their survivors are eligible.

During a typical month in 1973 about 10,000 eligible applicants received benefits under this act.

Benefits vary in amount, for disability it is about 66-2/3% of average weekly wage. Death benefits are 50% of weekly wage plust 16-2/3% for each surviving child. 66-2/3% is the maximum benefit.

For information contact:

Office of Workmen's Compensation Programs
Division of Longshoremen's and Harbor
   Worker's Compensation
Washington, D.C. 20211
(202) 382-1336

UNEMPLOYMENT INSURANCE

The Department of Labor administers a nationwide system of unemployment insurance. This program makes an important contribution to workers, employers, and the community. For the insured unemployed worker, there is money to help him through the time he is out of work. It gives workers a more secure feeling, knowing that if they should be laid off or unemployed they will not be totally without money.

About 80% of the nonagricultural workers are covered under this program. Railroad workers are covered by a separate railroad unemployment insurance law. Their coverage is explained in a section by itself.

A tax on payrolls is levied on specific employers, and an offset against that tax is allowed to employers for taxes paid under a State unemployment insurance law. Federal grants cover the State's cost in administering an approved law. All employers with 4 employees in at least 20 weeks of a year are taxes.

Each state determines eligibility requirements and amount of benefits. Benefits are related to the individuals past earnings. There are certain minimum and maximum limits. There is also a limit put on the number of weeks of unemployment in a year for which you may receive benefits. A worker must have a substantial amount of employment covered by the program to be eligible.

These are the basic requirements, in most states, that a worker must fulfill to be eligible.

To draw benefits an individual must 1) be ready and willing to work, 2) register for work at a public employment office, 3) must not have left his previous job without good cause, 4) must not be unemployed due to labor dispute (strike).

Benefits are paid as a matter or right. You may appeal if you think you have been denied benefits unfairly or if you think your amount is less than it should be.

For specific information, contact the Unemployment Office in your city, because each state has its own laws regarding unemployment insurance.

DEPARTMENT OF LABOR

Unemployment Insurance coverage is available to workers through Federal and State cooperation. States operate their own unemployment insurance programs. The Federal government finances the administration costs. To pay benefits, states rely solely on their own unemployment insurance tax collections. The Federal unemployment tax collections provide the funds with which the administration expenses are financed.

Applicants eligible are State unemployment insurance agencies. Eligible beneficiaries include 1) all workers whose employer contribute to the State unemployment insurance programs 2) Federal civilian employees 3) ex-servicemen if they are involuntarily unemployed but ready and able and meet the earning requirements of state law. There are individual State requirements that vary. By contacting the local employment office in your city you can find out these requirements.

The range of assistance is between $1,123,548 to $55,975,522.

Some statistics indicating the benefits paid and amount of unemployment taxes collected will show what this program accomplished. In fiscal year 1973 unemployment insurance taxes collected $4,634,192,000; benefits paid $4,795,322. Fiscal year 1974; estimated unemployment insurance taxes collected $4,600,000,000; benefits paid $5,043,313,000. Fiscal year 1975: estimated unemployment insurance taxes collected $4,600,000,000; benefits paid $6,516,131,000.

For further information contact: Local office of the

state employment service; local office of the State Unemployment Insurance Service or Headquarters Office:

> Associated Manpower Administrator
> Unemployment Insurance Service
> Manpower Administration
> U.S. Department of Labor
> Washington, D.C. 20210
> (202) 961-2701

Regional Offices Labor Department

Region I	*Address/Telephone*
Massachusetts, New Hampshire, Maine, Rhode Island, Vermont, Connecticut	John F. Kennedy Federal Bldg. Boston, Massachusetts 02203 (617) 223-543
Region II	
New York, New Jersey	1515 Broadway New York, New York 10036 (2120 971-7051

Region III	Address/Telephone
Pennsylvania, Virginia, Washington, D.C., Maryland, West Virginia, Delaware	3535 Market St. Philadelphia, Pennsylvania 19104 (215) 597-1116
Region IV	
Kentucky, Alabama, Florida, South Carolina, North Carolina, Mississippi, Tennessee, Georgia	1371 Peachtree St. N.E. Atlanta, Georgia 30309 (404) 526-5366
Region V	
Michigan, Ohio, Wisconsin, Minnesota, Illinois, Indiana	230 S. Dearborn St. Chicago, Illinois 60604 (312) 353-4122
Region VI	
Louisiana, Arkansas, Texas, Oklahoma, New Mexico	1100 Commerce St. Dallas, Texas 75202 (214) 749-3842

Region VII	*Address/Telephone*
Kansas, Missouri, Nebraska, Iowa	911 Walnut St. Kansas City, Missouri 64106 (816) 374-5941
Region VIII	
Colorado, Montana, North Dakota, South Dakota, Utah, Wyoming	1961 Stout St. Denver, Colorado 80202 (303) 837-3791
Region IX	
California, Hawaii, Nevada, Arizona	450 Golden Gate Ave. San Francisco, California 94102 (415) 556-8754
Region X	
Oregon, Washington, Idaho, Alaska	1321 2nd Ave. Seattle, Washington 98101 (206) 442-1545

CHAPTER V

U.S. DEPARTMENT OF THE INTERIOR

WHAT IS THE U.S. DEPARTMENT OF THE INTERIOR?

This executive department of the government which is divided into these main sections: Bureau of Indian Affairs, Bureau of Land Management, Bureau of Mines, Bureau of Reclamation, Bureau of Outdoor Recreation, The Geological Survey and the National Park Service, protects our resources.

HOW I CAN GET MONEY FROM THE U.S. DEPARTMENT OF THE INTERIOR

Loans and grants are available from several bureaus which are part of this department. They are the Bureau of Indian Affairs, Bureau of Commercial Fisheries and the Geological Survey. Eligibility requirements vary with the type of loan you apply for. More detailed information is given in the following sections.

U.S. DEPARTMENT OF INTERIOR

Bureau of Indian Affairs. This element of the U.S. Department of the Interior works to maximize Indian economic self-sufficiency, full participation of Indians in American life, and equal rights and privileges of citizenship for Indians.

The actual duties and services of this bureau include 1) acting as trustees for Indian land and money held in trust by the United States, 2) assist them in making effective use of their land and resources, 3) provides public services such as education and welfare aid, 4) guidance to those who want to leave the reservation area, 5) development of programs which lead to Indian responsibility of their own land and management, and 6) assistance in cooperation with Indians and local and state agencies, development of programs to attract Indians to reservation areas.

Those who may apply for funds under the program offered by the Bureau of Indian Affairs include Indians, Eskimos, and Aleuts.

Contact the Indian Agency superintendent.

Geological Survey. This groupp is responsible for the following functions; 1) classification of Federal land, 2) supervises mining oil and gas leases, 3) making surveys and investigations to determine the geologic structure of the U.S. and its territories, 4) preparing and publishing maps, 5) resolve problems of accuracy in name usage, and 6) determine quality, quantity, source distribution movement and availability of surface and ground waters.

Funds are available to individuals, partnerships and corporations for domestic mineral exploration.

For information:

> Office of Minerals Exploration
> Geological Survey
> U.S. Department of the Interior
> Washington, D.C.

Bureau of Commercial Fisheries. The following services are offered 1) market news service for the collection and publication of information on fishery commodities, 2) surveys to collect, analyze and publish statistics on production, prices, processing storage, and marketing of fishery products.

Loans and grants are available for financing and refinancing of operations, maintenance, replacement, repair, and equipment. Also, research and administration of fishing vessel, mortgage insurance program may be funded under this program.

For more information contact regional and area offices of Bureau of Commercial Fisheries. A directory is included following this section. Also the headquarters office.

Bureau of Commercial Fisheries
U.S. Department of the Interior
Washington, D.C. 20240

REGIONAL AND AREA OFFICES BUREAU OF COMMERCIAL FISHERIES

Region or Area	Address
Pacific	Arcade Building Seattle, Washington
Gulf and South Atlantic	Box 6245 St. Petersburg Beach, Florida
North Atlantic	Post Office Building Glouster, Mass. 01930
Great Lakes and Central	5 Research Drive Ann Arbor, Michigan 48103
Alaska	Juneau Daries Building Juneau, Alaska 99801

Pacific Southwest

Hawaii Area

101 Seaside Avenue
Terminal Island, California

2570 Dole Street
Honolulu, Hawaii

CHAPTER VI

ACTION

YOU CAN GET MONEY BEING A
SENIOR VOLUNTEER

Retired Senior Volunteer Program. This program works to establish a wide variety of community volunteer service opportunities for people 60 years old or older. They can therefore establish a recognized role in the community feeling they are doing a meaningful worthwhile service.

Project grants are offered to established community service organizations (either public or private non-profit) so they may assist in the development or operation (or both) of locally organized senior volunteer programs run by a competent staff. This local community service organization is responsible for the development of a great number of volunteer service opportunities in the community. The services may be connected with hospitals, day care centers, schools, libraries, and various other centers in the community. A local program also arranges for meals and transportation as needed.

Applicants eligible are public or private non-profit organizations. Beneficiaries eligible are men and women 60 years of age or older.

In fiscal year 1973, for instance, 510 senior volunteer programs were developed to support the activities of almost 100,000 senior volunteers.

For regional or local offices contact State Office on Aging located in the state capital also the regional offices of ACTION through the Coordinator of the Older Americans Volunteer Programs.

Headquarter Office is:

> Retired Senior Volunteer Program
> ACTION
> 806 Connecticut Ave. N.W.
> Washington, D.C. 20525
> (202) 254-7310

HOW TO GET MONEY BEING A FOSTER GRANDPARENT

For information on the Foster Grandparent program write to the above address. You will receive the latest facts and figures.

Regional Offices Action

Region I	Address/Telephone
Massachusetts, New Hampshire, Maine, Rhode Island, Vermont, Connecticut	John W. McCormack Federal Bldg. Boston, Massachusetts 02109 (617) 223-4297
Region II	
New York, New Jersey	26 Federal Plaza New York, New York 10007 (212) 264-2900
Region III	
Pennsylvania, Virginia, Washington, D.C., Maryland, West Virginia, Delaware	320 Walnut Street Philadelphia, Pennsylvania 19106 (215) 597-0732
Region IV	
Kentucky, Alabama, Florida, South Carolina, North Carolina, Mississippi, Tennessee, Georgia	730 Peachtree Street N.E. Atlanta, Georgia 30308 (404) 526-3337

Region V	*Address/Telephone*
Michigan, Ohio, Wisconsin, Minnesota, Illinois, Indiana	1 North Wacker Dr. Chicago, Illinois 60606 (312) 353-5107

Region VI

Louisiana, Arkansas, Texas, Oklahoma, New Mexico	212 North St. Paul Street Dallas, Texas 75201 (214) 749-1361

Region VII

Kansas, Missouri, Nebraska, Iowa	4th and State Streets Kansas City, Kansas 66101 (816) 374-4486

Region VIII

Colorado, Montana, North Dakota, South Dakota, Utah, Wyoming	1050-17th Street Denver, Colorado 80202 (303) 837-2671

Region IX

California, Hawaii, Nevada, Arizona	100 McAllister Street San Francisco, California 94102 (415) 556-1736

Region X	Address/Telephone
Oregon, Washington, Idaho, Alaska	1601 2nd Avenue Seattle, Washington 98101 (206) 442-1558

CHAPTER VII

RAILROAD RETIREMENT BOARD

Social Insurance for Railroad Workers. This program provides partial protection against loss of income for the Nation's railroad workers and their families. This loss of income may be the result of retirement, death, unemployment or sickness of the wage earner.

Those who are eligible for benefits under the Railroad Unemployment Insurance Act and the Railroad Unemployment Act are 1) workers who retire because of age or disability 2) eligible spouses of retired employees 3) surviving widows, widowers, children, and parents of deceased employed 4) unemployed workers 5) workers who are sick or injured.

Besides these benefits the Railroad Retirement Board participates in the administration of the Federal Health Insurance Program for the aged and disabled. This program covers railroad retirement beneficiaries and aged railroad employees the same as other aged persons.

To be eligible an employee must 1) have 10 or more years or railroad service for himself and his wife 2) have been injured at death for his survivors to be eligible for benefits 3) have earned at least $1,000 in railroad wages or 4) be a new employee having at least 7 months in a calendar (base) year to be a qualified employee in the applicable benefit year.

Supplemental annuities for long term employees averages $66.00 monthly with $70.00 being the maximum. For disability the average is $287.00 with the maximum being $587.00. Age annuities average $301.00 and $587.00 is the maximum. Wife's benefits average $141.00 and Widow's $183.00, while unemployment and sickness average $63.00 per week with the weekly maximum $63.50. Widowed mother's average $219.00 and children's average monthly benefit is $156.00 with $371.00 being the maximum.

CHAPTER VIII
VETERANS ADMINISTRATION

WHAT IS THE VETERANS ADMINISTRATION

In 1930, an independent agency known as the Veterans Administration was begun to protect the interest of nearly 30 million U.S. veterans of military service. It administers educational, housing and other benefits besides operating a medical system that incorporated 171 hospitals in 1976.

The headquarters is located at this address:

Veterans Administration
810 Vermont Avenue N.W.
Washington, D.C. 20420
(202) 393-4120

HOW I CAN COLLECT MONEY FROM THE VETERANS ADMINISTRATION?

Millions of dollars are lost each year because veterans, their families and survivors don't know about the benefits the V.A. has to offer, or how to obtain them.

Money is available for education, job training, medical care, pension, or buying a home, just to name some.

Eligibility varies, but in most cases, you have to have 6 months of continuous active service any part of which was after January 31, 1955 and before January 1, 1977 and not have been dishonorably discharged. You may also qualify if you were disabled as a result of military service and discharged with less than six months' service.

To apply contact your nearest Veterans Administration office. There is a directory of regional offices in this book following the section on Veterans Benefits.

Some of the major benefits and rights are discussed in detail. Read this section carefully to find out how and where to apply for your cash benefits.

DEPARTMENT OF VETERANS BENEFITS

Non-service Connected Disability Pension. This pension is paid to veterans who served during wartime or specified conflict periods. The veteran must be permanently and completely disabled from a non-service related injury, accident or illness. The disability cannot be willfully self-inflicted or the result of a dangerous health habit. This program offers subsistance support to veterans incapable of providing for their own basic needs.

To be eligible a veteran must have served 90 days or more during World War I, World War II, the Korean Conflict Period, or the Vietnam Era, or have left the armed forces before serving 90 days during one of the previously mentioned periods due to a service related disability. Any veteran of a qualifying wartime period who has reached age 65 is eligible to receive benefits.

To receive pension benefits the veteran cannot earn more than $2,600 per year if single of $3,800 per year if he has dependents. The veteran also cannot have an estate capable of supporting his existance.

The monthly pension ranges from $28 for a single veteran with a yearly income of more than $2,300 but less than $2,600 to a monthly income of $164 for a veteran benefits are also available if the veterans disability requires regular aid and attendance or renders the veteran housebound. The additional benefits are $110 and $44 per month respectively.

For more information cantact your regional office. Addresses and phone numbers listed in the directory at the end of this section or write headquarters office:

Veterans Administration Central Office
810 Vermont Avenue N.W.
Washington, D.C. 20420
(202) 393-4120

Veterans Compensation for Service Connected Disability. This program includes veterans dating back to the Spanish-American War with Service connected disability.

To be eligible for this compensation a veteran must have been disabled by injury or disease incurred or aggravated by active wartime or peacetime military service. The veteran must also have been discharged or separated from the service under other than dishonorable conditions.

The disability compensation payments distinguish between wartime and peacetime disabilities. Veterans eligible for wartime disability benefits receive monthly payments ranging from $28 to $495 based on the degree of disability with specific rates to $1,000.

Veterans whose wartime disabilities are rated at 50% or above are eligible for additional allowances for dependents.

The current wartime rates are listed below:

Wife and Dependency	100% Disability Wartime Rate	Monthly 50%	Payment 60%	By Degree of Disability 70%	80%	90%
Wife Only	$31	$16	$19	$22	$25	$28
Wife & One Child	$53	$27	$32	$37	$42	$47
Wife & Two Children	$67	$34	$41	$47	$54	$60
Wife & Three Children	$83	$42	$50	$59	$67	$75
Each Additional Child	$15	$15	$15	$15	$15	$15
No Wife & One Child	$21	$12	$13	$15	$17	$19
No Wife & Two Children	$36	$18	$22	$25	$29	$32
No Wife & Three Children	$53	$27	$32	$37	$42	$48

Each Additional Child	$15	$15	$15	$15	$15	$15
One Dependent Parent	$25	$13	$15	$18	$20	$23
Two Dependent Parents	$50	$25	$30	$35	$40	$45

Chronic Disease Presumption for Wartime or Peacetime Disability Compensation. Any veteran with active service after February 1, 1955 who develops a chronic disease to a degree of 10 percent or more disability within one (1) year of release or separation from service may be presumed to be service-connected for disability compensation. The presumptive period for tuberculosis or leprosy is 3 years. The period for multiple sclerosis is seven (7) years.

Veterans eligible for disability compensation resulting from peacetime service in the armed forces are entitled to monthly payments at 80% of the previously stated wartime rates. The peacetime rates range from $18 to $320 based on the degree of disability. Additional statutory awards are made for amputation, blindness and other disabilities up to a maximum of $800.

If the disability resulted from extra-hazardous

108

peacetime duty such as simulated war games the veteran may receive the wartime compensation rates. Peacetime veterans whose disabilities are rated at 50% or above may also be entitled to dependent compensation for wives, children and parents.

Any disability benefit received from Social Security for disability will not be reduced because of any service-connected disability compensation received from the Veterans Administration.

For more information contact your regional office. Addresses and phone numbers listed in the directory at the end of this section or write headquarters office:

Veterans Administration Central Office
810 Vermont Avenue N.W.
Washington, D.C. 20420
(202) 393-4120

Veterans Educational Assistance. This program offers financial assistance to veterans and servicemen who wish to further their education.

To bc eligible a veteran must have served on active duty for more than 180 continuous days and at least one day of his service must have occurred after January 31, 1955. The veteran must have been released under conditions other than dishonorable or discharged because of a service-connected disability. Any serviceman currently on active duty with over 180 days service is also eligible for the program.

The 181 day active service requirement excludes any time the serviceman spent assigned by the armed forces to a civilian institution for an educational course similar to a course offered to the general public or attended a service academy.

The range of institutions a serviceman can attend under this program extends from elementary school through the university level.

The serviceman can select any field of study the approved educational institution finds him qualified to undertake. Upon request the Veterans Administration will provide vocational counseling.

Each eligible person is entitled to educational assistance for a period 1-½ months for each month of his active service after January 31, 1955 but not more than 36 months. Veterans must begin this program within eight (8) years after their release from the service.

The program also offers tutorial assistance for veterans or servicemen involved in an above high school level educational program on at least a half-time basis. Tutorial payments are restricted to $50 per month and to a maximum amount of $450. These payments are not charged against the basic entitlement.

The educational assistance allowance cannot be paid to any eligible person on active duty whose education is paid for by the armed forces or Department of Health, Education and Welfare. The veteran also cannot be a Federal Government employee receiving his full salary and having his education paid for by the Government Employers' Training Act.

The following table displays the amount of monthly Educational Assistance benefits payable based on the amount of education being pursued and the family status of the veteran or serviceman:

| Type or Program | Amount of Monthly Assistance | | | |
	No Dependents	One Dependent	Two Dependents	Each Extra Dependent
Institutional:				
Full Time	$270	$321	$366	$22
Three Quarter Time	$203	$240	$275	$17
Half Time	$135	$160	$182	$11
Cooperative	$217	$255	$289	$17

A dependent can be a wife, child or parent of an eligible veteran.

A cooperative program is defined as a full time program of education which consists of institutional courses and alternate phases of training in a business or industrial establishment with the training in the business or industrial establishment being strictly supplemental to the institutional portion.

For more information contact your regional office. Addresses and phone numbers listed in the directory at the end of this seciton or write headquarters office:

Veterans Administration Central Office
810 Vermont Avenue N.W.
Washington, D.C. 20420
(202) 393-4120

Burial Expenses for Deceased Veterans of the Spanish-War, World War I, World War II, the Korean Conflict, the Vietnam Era and certain peacetime service.

To be eligible, the veteran cannot have received a discharge under dishonorable conditions. The veteran must also have served during a wartime, or during the Korean Conflict, or during the Vietnam Era. A veteran who served during peacetime but received a service-connected compensation at the time of his death, discharge or retirement from the service is also eligible to receive a burial expense benefit.

To receive the burial expense benefit a claim must be filed within two years after the deceased veteran's burial or cremation. Only the person who bore the veteran's burial expense or an undertaker, if unpaid, is eligible to receive the burial exppense benefit of up to $250. An additional $150 for interment or plot expenses is also granted if the veteran is not buried in a National Cemetary. If the veteran's death was service-connected the total benefit for burial expenses and interment is increased to $800. Transportation costs may also be allowed if death occurs while the veteran was in a V.A. hospital or home, or had his hospital or domicilary care paid by the V.A., or was in transit at V.A. expense at the time of this death.

For more information contact your regional office. Addresses and phone numbers listed in the directory at the end of this section or write headquarters office:

Veterans Administration Central Office
810 Vermont Avenue N.W.
Washington, D.C. 20420
(202) 393-4120

Compensation for Service-Connected Deaths for Veterans' Dependents. This program offers compensation for survivors of deceased veterans who served during or after the Spanish-American War and who died because of a service-connected cause which did not result from willful misconduct. The veteran must also have died before January 1, 1957 to qualify for this program.

Death compensation payments are payable to widows who have not remarried, unmarried children under 18 (or under 23 if attending a V.A. approved school), helpless children and dependent parents.

If the veteran was discharged from the service prior to service-connected death, the veteran's discharge cannot have been under dishonorable conditions.

Widows, children, or parents eligible for this program can exercise a one time option to receive Veterans' Dependency and Indemnity Compensation payments but once that option is exercised it can never be reversed.

Veterans who have died of a service-connected cause on or after May 1, 1957 and were not covered by the Veterans' Dependency and Indemnity Compensation program may receive a one time death compensation payment under this program.

The monthly compensation paid to dependents ranges from $67 per month paid to one dependent child to $122 per month paid to three dependent children. Beyond the above stated range each additional child of an eligible widow beyond the stated range is paid $29 per month and each additional dependent child with no widow receives $23 per month. An additional payment of $55 per month is allowable if a widow or dependent parent is in need of continuing aid or assistance.

For more information contact your regional office. Addresses and phone numbers listed in the directory at the end of this section or write headquarters office:

Veterans Administration Central Office
810 Vermont Avenue N.W.
Washington, D.C. 20420
(202) 393-4120

Veterans Dependency and Indemnity Compensation for Service-Connected Death. This program became effective January 1, 1957 and replaced the program entitled "Compensation for Service-Connected Deaths for Veterans' Dependents." As with the previous program this program offers compensation for survivors of deceased veterans who died because of service-connected causes which did not result from willful misconduct. To be eligible for this program the veteran must have died on or after January 1, 1957 unless the veteran's dependents have exercised their option to switch to this program from the Compensation for Service-Connected Deaths for Veterans Dependents program.

Death compensation payments are payable to widows who have not remarried, unmarried children under 18 (or 23 if attending a V.A. approved school), helpless children and dependent parents.

The monthly compensation paid to dependents ranges from $92 per month paid to one child no widow to $503 paid to a widow whose deceased spouse had attained the highest military pay grade. Beyond the stated range of payments each child of a dependent widow is entitled to an additional $22 per month. An additional payment of $55 per month is granted if the widow or dependent parent is in need of continuing aid or assistance.

For more information contact your regional office. Addresses and phone numbers listed in the directory at the end of this section or write headquarters office:

Veterans Administration Central Office
810 Vermont Avenue N.W.
Washington, D.C. 20420
(202) 393-4120

Widows and Children of Veterans Non-service Connected Death Pension. This pension is payable to the widows and children of veterans who served during wartime or the Korean Conflict period. The veteran must also have died of causes unrelated to his military service.

This pension system is divided into two programs. The first is termed the prior system and the second is termed the current pension system.

The prior pension system covers widows and children who came onto the pension rolls on or before June 30, 1960.

The current pension system covers widows and children who came on the pension rolls on or after July 1, 1960.

Anyone covered under the prior pension system can exercise an option to switch to the current pension system but once this choice is made it cannot be reversed. Anyone who became eligible for this pension on or after July 1, 1960 must participate in the current pension plan.

The eligibility requirements of the prior pension system vary slightly depending upon which war the veteran served with the armed forces. The eligibility requirements common to all wars are that the veteran must have had at least 90 days service during a war, unless he was discharged prior to 90 days because of a service-connected disability. The veteran also must have been discharged under conditions other than dishonorable. If you fail to meet these general requirements you may still receive a pension or you meet the additional requirements established for each wartime period. Contact your regional Department of Veterans Benefits, Veterans Administrations and request eligibility requirements for the wartime period of specific interest to you.

The prior pension system offers payment to widows and unmarried children of veterans under age 18. Any child attending a V.A. approved school can continue to receive benefits until age 21. Any child permanently incapable of self-support due to a mental or physical defect which occurred prior to age 18 can continue to receive pension as long as the condition exists or until they marry.

The monthly payments for widows and children of veterans who served in the Spanish-American War are as follows:

	Payment For Month
Widow Only	$70.00
Widow, If Wife During Service	$75.00
Widow, With Veteran's Children: Additional Amount For Each Child	$ 8.13
No Widow, One Child	$73.13
Additional Amount For Each Additional Child	$ 8.13
Additional Amount If Regular Aid Or Attendance Required	$55.00

The monthly payments for widows and children of veterans who served in World War I, World War II, or the Korean Conflict are as follows:

	Payment For Month
Widow Only	$50.40
Widow, 1 Child	$63.00
Each Additional Child	$ 7.56
No Widow, 1 Child	$27.30

No Widow, 2 Children	$40.95
No Widow, 3 Children	$54.60
Each Additional Child	$ 7.56

The prior pension system limits the income a widow can earn from other sources to $2,200 per year except there is no income limitation for widows of Spanish-American War veterans. If a widow of World War I, World War II or Korean War Conflict has one or more children of the veteran the income limitation is increased to $3,500 annually. If there is no widow or if the widow does not qualify for pension benefits the children of the World War I, World War II, or Korean Conflict veteran may qualify for pension if their income from other sources does not exceed $2,200 per year.

The current pension system does not affect widows or children of veterans of the Spanish-American War. This system covers widows and children of World War I, World War II, Korean Conflict, or Vietnam Era. The veteran must have had 90 days service unless discharged sooner due to a service-connected disability, or he must have been receiving or entitled to receive compensation or retirement benefits for a service-connected disability incurred during the war, and must have been discharged under conditions other than dishonorable.

The current pension system offers payment to widows and unmarried children of veterans under age 18. Any child attending a V.A. approved school can continue to receive benefits until age 21. Any child permanently incapable of self-suppport due to a mental or physical defect which occurred prior to age 18 can continue to receive pension as long as the condition exists or until they marry.

The pension a widow with no eligible children receives from the current pension system varies with the amount of her income from other sources. If the widow's annual income from other sources were $300 or less, her monthly pension would be $96. As the widows annual income increases the amount of the monthly pension decreases. The minimum pension is $21 per month and a widow of any income level above $2,600 per year is eligible for this pension. The pension for a widow with one child of a veteran is $114 per month if the widow's income from other sources does not exceed $700 annually. As the widows annual income increases the pension amount decreases. The minimum pension of $44 per month is paid when the widow's income from other sources reaches $3,800 per year. If a widow's income from other cources exceeds $3,800 she receives no pension. If a widow has more than one child the monthly pension payment is increased by $18 for each additional child.

If there is no widow (or if the widow is ineligible), the eligible children of veterans receive the following pension:

> One Child $44 Per Month
>
> $18 Per Month is Added For Each Additional Child

If the child has income other than from his own earnings which exceeds $2,000 per year, no pension will be paid. Also, no pension is paid to any widow or child whose estates are large enough to provide their maintenance.

For more information contact your regional office. Addresses and phone numbers listed in the directory at the end of this section or write headquarters office:

> Veterans Administration Office
> 810 Vermont Avenue N.W.
> Washington, D.C. 20420
> (202) 393-4120

VETERANS ADMINISTRATION LOANS

Type	Use	Applicants	Where To Apply
Real Estate Loans	Buy, build, repair home in which he lives or will live; buy land, build, repair, improve buildings for farm operation	World War II, Korena Conflict, post-Korean veterans, servicemen with 2 years active duty	Bank or private lender after V.A. Office approves eligibility.
Real Estate Loans for Business	Buy land or buy, repair, build; or improve buildings used in operating a business	World War II and Korean Conflict veterans	Bank or private lender after V.A. Office approves eligibility
Farm Operation Loans	Buy property other than real estate (supplies, machinery, equipment) or for working capital	World War II, Korean Conflict, post-Korean veterans, servicemen with 2 years active duty	Bank or private lender after V.A. Office approves eligibility
Business Loans	Buy property other than real estate (inventory, equipment, machinery) or for working capital	World War II, Korean Conflict veterans	Bank or private lender after V.A. Office approves eligibility

Type	Use	Applicants	Where To Apply
Housing Credit Shortage Loans	For housing in certain designated housing credit shortage areas (Direct Loans	World War II, Korean Conflict, post-Korean veterans, servicemen with 2 years active duty	V.A. Office nearest area with shortage

CHAPTER IX

U.S. OFFICE EDUCATION

IF YOU ARE A STUDENT
YOU CAN COLLECT MONEY

Through the United States Office of Education in Washington, D.C. there are a number of programs available including vocational training and college loans and grants.

The Basic Educational Opportunity Grant Program. Under Title IV of the Higher Education Act of 1965 educational opportunity grants will be made to help college students with exceptional financial needs. In past years large amounts of cash have gone unclaimed. For instance, in 1974, $135,000,000 went unclaimed.

National Direct Student Loan Program. These loans are offered directly to students with 10 years to repay the amount borrowed at 3%. About $321,000,000 is offered each year under this program.

Work Study Program. Through this program students have a chance to earn up to $3.50 per hour while in school.

The Guaranteed Student Loan Program. Students may borrow thousands of dollars each year they are in school. The federal government guarantees the loan. The interest rate is 7% with ten years to repay it.

The Supplemental Education Opportunity Grant Program. Under this particular plan, students may obtain funds if their school matches the amount they are given with money from the state or another source. This program has $240,000,000 to give away.

This money is here for you. For more information on where to apply or who is eligible write:

> U.S. Office of Education
> Washington, D.C. 20201

CHAPTER X

NATIONAL FOUNDATION OF THE ARTS AND HUMANITIES

IF YOU ARE A DANCER OR CHOREOGRAPHER YOU CAN GET MONEY FROM THE U.S. GOVT.

Promotion of the Arts

Dance. Project grants are offered to assist dancers, choreographer and dance organization. They may be used 1) to create workshops 2) tours 3) criticism 4) improve management 5) national services 6) dance films and 7) regional development. Funds may not be used to construct or renovate facilities or for scholarships, study abroad, research or publications.

Those eligible include organizations that are nonprofit with donations qualifying as charitable deductions (under Section 170C of the Internal Revenue Code.)

These organizations include State and local government and State art agencies.

In most cases grants are awarded to United States citizens who by law must be of exceptional talent.

Assistance varies for individuals between $1,200 and $22,400 and for organizations between $1,200 and $176,250. 125 organizations and 95 individuals received grants in the fiscal year 1973.

For more information write:

Director of Dance Programs
National Endowment for the Arts
Washington, D.C. 20506
(202) 382-5853

IF YOU ARE INVOLVED IN PUBLIC MEDIA THE U.S. GOVERNMENT HAS MONEY FOR YOU

Promotion of the Arts

Public media. Grants are available for 1) programming (for public media arts), 2) experimental projects in film, videotape, or sound recording, 3) assistance for regional film centers, educational institutions for development of film course cirricula, seminar sponsorship, in service training for film teachers. Funds are not available for construction and renovation of facilities for public media.

To be eligible organizations must be nonprofit with donations qualifying as charitable deductions (according to Internal Revenue Code, Section 170C0.

These organizations include state and local governments and state art agencies.

In most cases, grants are awarded to United States citizens of exceptional talent (by law).

Organizations received between $750 and $60,000 while individuals ranged from $1,500 to $11,665. Grants in fiscal year 1973 were awarded to 85 organizations and 9 individuals.

For additional information contact:

Director, Public Media Program
National Endowment for the Arts
Washington, D.C. 20506
(202) 382-6178

IF YOU ARE AN ARTIST, DANCER, MUSICIAN, EDUCATOR, THEATER GROUP OR IN A RELATED FIELD YOU CAN GET MONEY FROM THE U.S. GOVERNMENT

Promotion of the Arts

Education. Grants are offered for special innovation programs in arts education. These grants may be used to 1) place professional artists in elementary or secondary schools, 2) projects that bring professional artists and young people together in arts activities in other than the traditional school environment, 3) funds are not used for rehabilitation or construction of facilities.

To be eligible applicants may be nonprofit organizations with donations qualifying as charitable deductions (under Section 170C of the Internal Revenue Code). These organizations include state and local governments and state art agencies.

In most cases grants are awarded to United States citizens who by law must be of exceptional talent.

Organizations received between $2,000 and $85,000 from this program. In the fiscal year 1973, 179 organizations received grants.

For information contact:

Director for Education Program
National Endowment for the Arts
Washington, D.C. 20506
(202) 382-6196

IF YOU ARE A PAINTER, SCULPTOR, PHOTOGRAPHER, PRINTMAKER OR CRAFTSMAN THE U.S. GOVERNMENT HAS MONEY FOR YOU

Promotion of the Arts

Visual. Grants are available 1) to provide assistance to individual painters, sculptors, printmakers, art critics, photographers and craftsmen who have exceptional talent, 2) for commissioning and placement of art works in public places, 3) for short-term residencies of artists, critics, craftsmen and photographers in educational and cultural institutions, 4) for workshops, 5) visual arts in the performing arts and 6) artists' services.

To be eligible organizations must be nonprofit with donations qualifying as charitable deductions (under Section 170C of the Internal Revenue Code). These organizations include state, local governments and state art agencies. In most cases these grants are awarded to United States citizens who by law must be of exceptional talent.

204 individuals and 174 organizations received grants in fiscal year 1973.

The range of financial asistance to individuals was between $750 and $7,500 while for organizations it was between $600 and $50,00.

For additional information contact:

Director for Visual Arts Program
National Endowment for the Arts
Washington, D.C. 20506
(202) 382-7068

IF YOU ARE A WRITER YOU CAN GET MONEY FROM THE U.S. GOVERNMENT

Promotion of the Arts

Literature. Project grants for 1) the creation of new works or for bringing creative writers into elementary and secondary schools and developing colleges, 2) support of small literary magazines and presses, 3) international conferences of writers hosted in the United States.

Funds may not be used for construction or renovation of facilities or for the publication of completed works.

Those eligible may be nonprofit organizations with donations qualifying as charitable deductions (according to Section 170C of the Internal Revenue Code). These organizations include state and local governments and state art agencies. In most cases, individuals are awarded to United States citizens of exceptional talent.

In fiscal year 1973, 60 individuals and 20 organizations received grants. Amounts granted varied for organizations betweem $1.000 and $250,000.

For more information contact:

> Director, Literature Program
> National Endowment for the Arts
> Washington, D.C. 20506
> (201) 382-6186

IF YOU ARE A MUSICIAN, COMPOSER OR OPERA COMPANY, YOU CAN GET MONEY FROM THE U.S. GOVERNMENT

Promotion of the Arts

Music. Project grants are offered to assist symphony orchestras, opera companies, national audience development projects, contemporary music groups, composers and other groups that serve the field of music.

The funds may be used for 1) new works, 2) touring, 3) concert series expansion, 4) special music education projects, 5) forums, 6) institutes, 7) jazz, folk or ethnic musicians and organizations. Funds are not used for construction or renovation of facilities.

To be eligible, organizations must be nonprofit with donations qualifying as charitable deductions (under Section 170C of the Internal Revenue Code). These organizations include state, local governments and state art agencies. In most cases, these grants are awarded to United States citizens who by law must be of exceptional talent.

Grants range in amount from $190 to $200,000 for organizations and $150 to $10,000 for individuals. In fiscal year 1973, 261 organizations and 108 individuals were granted assistance under this program.

For further information contact:

> Director of Music Program
> National Endowment for the Arts
> Washington, D.C. 20506
> (202) 382-5755

IF YOU ARE INVOLVED IN ARCHITECTURE, LANDSCAPE ARCHITECTURE, OR ENVIRONMENTAL DESIGN THE U.S. GOVERNMENT HAS MONEY FOR YOU

Promotion of the Arts

Architecture and Environment Arts. Grants are provided for 1) research projects, 2) professional education projects, 3) and public awareness in architecture, landscape architecture and environmental design. No funds may be used for construction or renovation of facilities.

To be eligible, organizations must be nonprofit with donations qualifying as charitable deductions (under Section 170C of the Internal Revenue Code). These organizations include state, local governments and state art agencies. In most cases, these grants are awarded to United States citizens who by law must be of exceptional talent.

In fiscal year 1973, individuals received 61 grants and organizations 50. The amounts for individual grants ranged from $1,000 to $10,000 while organizations were between $2,600 and $60,000.

For more information contact:

> Director for Architecture and Environmental
> Arts Program
> National Endowment for the Arts
> Washington, D.C. 20506
> (202) 382-6657

IF YOU ARE A MEMBER OF A PROFESSIONAL THEATER COMPANY, YOU CAN GET MONEY FROM THE U.S. GOVERNMENT

Promotion of the Arts

Theater. These grants are offered to 1) professional theater companies, 2) professional experimental theater companies, 3) new play producing groups, 4) playwright development programs, 5) professional theater for children and youth, 6) and theater service organizations. There was no program to aid individual artists. Funds were not to be used for construction or renovation of facilities.

To be eligible, organizations must be nonprofit with donations qualifying as charitable deductions (under Section 170C of the Internal Revenue Code). These organizations include state, local governments and state art agencies.

Organizations received financial assistance ranging from $2,500 to $250,000. In 1973 fiscal year, 105 organizations received assistance.

For more information contact:

Director for Theater Program
National Endowment for the Arts
Washington, D.C. 20506
(202) 382-5763

Promotional Arts

Expansion Arts. Project grants are offered to art organizations that are professionally directed and community based. Funds may be used for 1) instruction and training projects on all levels, 2) production of original and promising works of art, 3) promotion of cross-cultural exchange, 4) creation of new ways to assimilate new forms with established forms, 5) involvement of the arts to help achieve educational and social goals.

To be eligible, organizations must be nonprofit with donations qualifying as charitable deductions (under Section 170C of the Internal Revenue Code). These organizations include state, local governments and state art agencies. In most cases, these grants are awarded to

United States citizens who by law must be of exceptional talent.

Funds received by organizations ranged from $2,000 to $50,000 with 196 organizations receiving assistance in the fiscal year 1973.

For more information, write or call:

Director for Expansion Arts Program
National Endowment for the Arts
Washington, D.C. 20506
(202) 382-6071

Promotion of the Arts

Special Projects. Grants are provided for a limited number of special projects that don't fit into any other endowment program or those that involve two or more art forms or program areas.

The funds may be used for 1) projects involving two or mroe forms, 2) projects involving two or more program areas. These projects must meet professional standards, have potential to reach national or regional significance.

To be eligible, organizations must be nonprofit with donations qualifying as charitable deductions (under Section 170C of the Internal Revenue Code). These organizations include state, local governments and state art agencies. In most cases, these grants are awarded to United States citizens who by law must be of exceptional talent.

For more information contact:

Director, Special Projects Program
National Endowment of the Arts
Washington, D.C. 20506
(202) 382-3765

Museums. Grants to support the activities of American museums. Funds may be used for 1) mounting special exhibitions, 2) utilization of collections, 3) visiting specialists, 4) conservation, 5) training museum ·professionals and 6) renovation.

To be eligible, organizations must be nonprofit with donations qualifying as charitable deductions (under Section 170C of the Internal Revenue Code). These organizations include stae, local governments and state art agencies. In most cases, these grants are awarded to United States citizens who by law must be of exceptional talent.

Amounts for individuals range from $1,200 to $9,000 and for organizations $500 to $125,000 (half Federal funds and half donations).

For more information, write or call:

Director for Museum Program
National Endowment for the Arts
Washington, D.C.
(202) 382-5928

CHAPTER XI

SMALL BUSINESS ADMINISTRATION

WHAT IS THE SMALL BUSINESS ADMINISTRATION?

The Small Business Administration is an independent agency of the U.S. Government. It was established in 1953 to extend loans to small firms that were not able to get credit from commercial banks. This agency also helps qualified small businesses get credit from commercial banks and win government contracts. In addition, it promotes research on small business problems.

HOW CAN I GET MONEY FROM THE SBA?

Through the business loan program of the Small

Business Administration credit-worthy small businesses can receive financing. If you want to purchase equipment and materials, expand or modernize your business or need working capital, contact your field office. The staffs of these offices are ready to be of all possible assistance. In the next section of this book the detailed information you need will be explained, so you can get the cash you need for your small business. If you don't find the information you need here, we include a directory of regional and headquarters office so you can get someone who can assist you in getting the money you need.

Small Business Investment Companies help stimulate and improve small business and the national economy. Eligible small businesses are provided with management and financial assistance on a continuing basis. The Small Business Investment Act was passed in 1958 and authorized the establishment of publicly owned and operated Small Business Investment Companies. The Small Business Administration licenses, regulates and helps finance these new organizations. Financial assistance is provided by making long-term loans to these small concerns and/or by purchase of debt or equity type securities issued by these firms.

To be eligible any chartered small business investment company that has 1) combined paid in capital and paid in surplus of not less than $150,000, 2) qualified management, 3) evidence of a sound operation. Guaranteed loans averaged between $20,000 and $5,000,000.

Other related programs include Economic Opportunity Loans for Small Businesses, Management Assistance to Small Businesses, Minority Buriness Development-Procurement Assistance and State or Local Development Company Loans.

For more information contact:

Small Business Administration
1441 L. Street N.W.
Washington, D.C. 20416
(202) 382-6444

Product Disaster Loans are granted to assist small businesses that have suffered financial loss because a product they manufactured was found unfit for human consumption (toxic).

Direct loans are offered at 5% for up to $500,000 with up to 30 years to repay. Funds can be used to pay liabilities that the business could have taken care of if the disaster did not occur. They can also be used for working capital and in some cases acquire equipment or facilities necessary to meet health or sanitary requirements to make a marketable product.

For declarations made between January 1, 1972, and June 30, 1973, the interest rate is 1%. A direct loan or Small Business Association share of an immediate participation loan is limited to $500,000 to any one small business or affiliated group of concerns. Additional amounts are available as guaranteed loans made by a financial institution.

The amount of financial assistance ranges from $200 to $250,000.

For more information contact:

> Office of Disaster Operations
> Small Business Administration
> 1441 L. Street N.W.
> Washington, D.C. 20416
> (202) 382-3175

Small Business Loans are granted to aid small businesses in financing needs. Funds may be used to 1) purchase equipment or materials, 2) for working capital,

3) to construct, expand or convert facilities. Gambling establishments, communications media, non-profit enterprises, lending or investment businesses, speculators in property and financing of real property held for sale or investment are excluded. They may not be used to indiscriminately relocate the business. In addition, funds must not be available at reasonable terms or used to pay off a loss to an unsecured creditor who may sustain a loss.

Those eligible are 1) small businesses that are independently owned and operated and is not dominant in its field, 2) for manufacturers average number of employees not to exceed 5 million dollars and 4) for retail and service concerns revenues not exceeding $1,000,000.

Direct and insured or guaranteed loans are available. The average direct loans ranged from $1,800 to $219,000 and the guaranteed from $1,500 to $929,000.

For more information contact the district office or the headquarters:

> Office of Financing
> Small Business Administration
> 1441 L. Street N.W.
> Washington, D.C. 20416
> (202) 382-4987

Physical Disaster Loans are provided to restore victims of a physical disaster to predisaster condition. These are direct loans at 5% interest rate available to anyone regardless of their ability to obtain needed funds from private sources. Depending upon the date of the disaster and the governing legislation the rate of interest varies. Loans are made for up to 30 years. Funds may be used to repair or replace damaged or destroyed reality, machinery, and equipment, household or personal property. However the funds must be used for the purpose stipulated in an authorization issued with each plan. Only those engaged in agriculture are not eligible nor may funds be used by an otherwise eligible borrower for agricultural purposes.

Requirements for eligibility include: suffered physical property loss resulting from a disaster which had occurred in an area designated as eligible for assistance by the Administration. This could be the result of flood, riot, civil disturbance or other disaster. Those eligible to apply for assistance include: individuals, businesses, churches, private schools, hospitals and colleges and universities.

During fiscal year 1972, there were 93,000 loans made.

For more information contact your field office or:

Office of Disaster Operations
Small Business Administration
1441 L. Street N.W.
Washington, D.C. 20416
(202) 382-3175

Management and Technical Assistance for Disadvantaged Businessmen. Management and technical assistance through public or private organizations is provided to existing or potential businessmen who are disadvantaged either economically or socially or who live in an area of high unemployment.

Projects that provide 1) planning and research 2) development of new businessmen, businesses and business opportunities and 3) counseling, management, training legal and related services receive financial assistance.

Public or private organizations that are capable of providing necessary assistance are eligible applicants. Businesses or potential businessmen who are economically or socially disadvantaged are eligible beneficiaries.

For more information contact your local Small Business Administration field office or the headquarters:

Office of Management Assistance
1441 L. Street N.W.
Washington, D.C. 20416
(202) 382-5344

Minority Business Development Procurement Assistance insures that businesses owned and controlled by disadvantaged persons participate in Federal Contracting and establishing small manufacturing service and construction businesses that may become independent and self-sustaining.

To be eligible you must be disadvantaged. These are people who have been deprived of the opportunity to develop and maintain a position in the economy because of social or economic disadvantage; this disadvantage being beyond their control

In fiscal year 1972, contracts to 992 disadvantaged companies were awarded contracts valued at $15,390,380.

For additional information contact your field office or headquarters:

Office of Business Development
Small Business Administration
1441 L. Street N.W.
Washington, D.C. 20416
(202) 382-6891

Lease Guarantees For Small Businesses enables small businesses to obtain lease by guaranteeing the rent payment. This applies to rental under new leases on real property entered into by small businesses. $2,500,000 is the maximum amount of aggregate rental under one lease can be guaranteed or $15,000 monthly (whichever is less).

To be eligible applicant must 1) be the owner of a small business 2) small business must be independently owned and operated and not dominant in its field 3) small business must meet the Small Business Administration size standards for financial assistance.

The range of financial assistance varies according to the nature of the business. It has been from $17,500 to $6,000,000.

Applicants should apply to the Small Business Administration field office for the location of the facility to be leased.

For additional information contact:

Office of Community Development
Small Business Administration
1441 L. Street N.W.
Washington, D.C. 20416
(202) 382-7041

149

Economic Opportunity Loans for Small Business provides loans up to $50,000 and management assistance to low-income or socially or economically disadvantaged persons for small businesses.

Funds must be used to 1) establish, serve and strengthen small businesses 2) this excludes communications media, non-profit enterprises, lending or investment enterprises, speculators in property and financing real property held for sale or investment 3) funds must not be obtainable from any other source at reasonable terms.

To be eligible applicants must 1) be low-income or economically or socially disadvantaged 2) be denied adequate financing elsewhere at reasonable terms.

Direct and insured loans are granted and range up to $50,000. In fiscal year 1972, over seven thousand loans were made.

For information contact:

Director
Office of Financing
Small Business Administration
1441 L. Street N.W.
Washington, D.C. 20416
(202) 382-4987

Economic Injury Disaster Loans. These funds assist businesses suffering economically because of Small Business Administration, Department of Agriculture, or Presidential disaster designations. Amounts up to $500,000 SBA share at 5% with up to 30 years to repay. They are offered to small businesses of groups of affiliated concerns. Funds can be provided to pay current liabilities which the firm could have paid if the disaster had not occurred. For a limited period of time it can be provided for working capital until business conditions return to normal Funds are not available for realty, or for buying or repairing equipment. The interest varies depending on the date of the disaster and the governing disaster legislation. A direct loan or SBA share of an immediate participation loan is limited to $500,000. Additional amounts are available as guaranteed loans made by a financial institution.

The direct loans range between $280 to $500,000. To be eligible the applicant must 1) be a small business as described according to the Small Business Administration rules and regulations 2) show evidence of the economic injury claimed and the extent of the damage.

For further information contact your field office or

headquarters office:

> Office of Disaster Operations
> Small Business Administration
> 1441 L. Street N.W.
> Washington, D.C. 20416
> (202) 382-3175

Displaced Business Loans. These loans are available to small businesses so they may continue in business, purchase a business or establish a new business if they have suffered a substantial economic injury as a result of displacement by or location in or near a federally aided project.

There are certain restrictions. For example, speculation and non-profit seeking enterprise selling business to strangers, paying off principals or unsecured creditors, holding real property for sale or investment (primarily), agricultural activity and monopoly are excluded. Personal and business assets must be used if at all feasible. There is no maximum loan amount. 30 years is the maturity and maximum time. The interest rate-bank share of the loan (legal and reasonable) is set quarterly. The SBA share is established by legislative formula annually.

To be an eligible applicant a small business must have suffered physical displacement and/or economic injury because of a federally aided urban renewal project or a construction or highway project.

In the fiscal year 1972, 336 loans were approved. Direct loans range from $2,000 to $1,300,000 and guaranteed from $33,000 to $513,000.

For additional help contact your regional or headquarters office:

Headquarters Office Is—
Director, Office of Financing
Small Business Administration
Washington, D.C. 20416
(202) 382-4987

SMALL BUSINESS ADMINISTRATION LOANS (FINANCIAL, COMMERCIAL, AND INDUSTRIAL)

Business Loans. Small firms may obtain funds for construction conversion or expansion, purchase of equipment, machinery, supplies, or materials. Loans may be obtained at nearest SBA field office. Direct loans or loans in participation with banks may be used to acquire working capital.

Economic Opportunity Loans. Funds to assist small businesses with marginal or below marginal incomes or those who have been denied equal opportunity are available by applying at nearest SBA field office. Low income disadvantaged persons who wish to establish small businesses or improve it may apply.

Economic Injury Loans. Funds are available to small firms suffering from economic injury due to 1) U.S. trade agreements, 2) major or natural disaster declared by President or Secretary of Agriculture, 3) Federally-aided urban renewal or highway construction program, 4) inability to market a product because of disease or toxicity. Applications may be made at nearest SBA office.

Development Company Loans. Funds are used to establish and finance the operation of State and local small business development companies. These companies make loans to small firms for expanison, conversion, and plant construction.

Small Business Investment Company Loans. Funds assist SBA licensed business investment companies which make loans to small businesses. Applicants may apply to Washington Office of Small Business Administration.

PRIVATE FINANCING INSTITUTIONS
(UNDER GOVERNMENT GUARANTEE)

Type	Funds Used For	Applicants	Where To Apply
Defense Production	To expedite the financing of persons having contracts necessary for national defense	Contractors, subcontractors, and others, doing business with the Government through the 1) Departments of Defense, Interior, Agriculture, Commerce, or 2) various agencies, ADC, GSA, NASA, Supply, or 3) Army, Navy, or Air Force	At a bank, which, applies through a Federal Reserve Bank to the appropriate Government department or agency for a guarantee of the loan

Regional Offices Small Business Administration

Region I	*Address/Telephone*
Massachusetts, New Hampshire, Maine, Rhode Island, Vermont, Connecticut	150 Causeway St.. Boston, Massachusetts 02114 (617) 223-6660
Region II	
New York, New Jersey	26 Federal Plaza New York, New York 10007 (212) 264-1318
Region III	
Pennsylvania, Virginia, Washington, D.C., Maryland, West Virginia, Delaware	1 Decker Square Bala Cynwyd, Pennsylvania 19004 (215) 597-3201
Region IV	
Kentucky, Alabama, Florida, South Carolina, North Carolina, Mississippi, Tennessee, Georgia	1401 Peachtree St. N.E. Atlanta, Georgia 30309 (404) 526-5749

Region V	*Address/Telephone*
Michigan, Ohio, Wisconsin, Minnesota, Illinois, Indiana	219 South Dearborn St. Chicago, Illinois 60604 (312) 353-4485
Region VI	
Louisiana, Arkansas, Texas, Oklahoma, New Mexico	1720 Regal Row Dallas, Texas 75325 (214) 749-1263
Region VII	
Kansas, Missouri, Nebraska, Iowa	911 Walnut St. Kansas City, Missouri 64106 (816) 374-3316
Region VIII	
Colorado, Montana, North Dakota, South Dakota, Utah, Wyoming	721-9th St. Denver, Colorado 80202 (303) 837-3673

Region IX	Address/Telephone
California, Hawaii, Nevada, Arizona	450 Golden Gate Ave. Box 36044 San Francisco, California 94102 (415) 556-7487
Region X	
Oregon, Washington, Idaho, Alaska	710 2nd Ave. Seattle, Washington 98104 (206) 442-7791

CHAPTER XII

FEDERAL COURTS

MONEY FROM THE FEDERAL COURTS

False Claims Act. Under the False Claims Act of 1863 a private citizen may bring a law suit against government contractors on the governments behalf if the contractor has acted fraudulently. You may collect up to 25% of the settlement. If you lose, however, it will cost you your time, energy and money. Make sure you have a solid case.

You are obliged to give the Justice Department the option of joining you in the suit. Suits brought against government contractors by private individuals, in the governments behalf, are called, qui tam suits.

159

CHAPTER XIII

U.S. DEPARTMENT OF H.U.D.

WHAT IS THE DEPARTMENT OF HOUSING AND URBAN DEVELOPMENT?

In 1965 this department of the government was created. Within the department are several agencies. They are the Federal Housing Administration, The Public Housing Administration, Housing and Home Finance Agency, The Federal National Mortgage Association and the Urban Renewal Administration.

Federal Housing Administration. Helps families undertake home ownership. Enables them to own a home within their means by paying monthly installments over a period of years.

The way the FHA does this, is to insure mortgage loans made by banks, building and loan associations, mortgage companies and other FHA approved lenders.

Housing and Home Finance Agency. This agency is responsible for the principle housing programs and functions of the Federal Government. These responsibilities include:

1) Supervision and coordination of its constituents.
2) Approval and Certification of workable programs for community improvement.
3) Administration of the urban studies and housing research program.
4) Administration of the low-income housing program.

Housing Loans and Mortgage Insurance. There are about 10 types of loans for housing under this description they maybe used for 1) financing repairs and improvements to homes and other property and for the building of new small nonresidential structures, 2) purchase of new or existing 1 to 4 family dwellings, mobile homes or to refinance deabts on existing housing, 3) insurance of and interest reduction payments on mortgage loans for new or existing 1 family dwellings by lower income families, 4) insurance of and interest reduction payments on mortgage loans to finance renovation of housing for low income families, 5) insurance of mortgage loans for multifamily rental and co-op housing and mobile home courts, 6) for insurance of mortgage loans for rental housing for the elderly or physically handicapped, 7) rent supplements to help provide decent housing in multifamily dwellings, 8) insurance of and reduction of payments on mortgage loans for rental and cooperative housing for lower income families, 9) temporary loans and contributions for development and operation of low-rent public housing projects, 10) college housing loans and debt service grants to construct housing for students, faculty, student nurses or interns.

For the loans described 1 thru 8 apply at the Federal Housing Administration office. Loans 9 and 10 may be applied for at the Housing and Urban Development Area or regional office.

Other loans for Medical Care facilities may be applied for at the Federal Housing Administration. They may be FHA insurance of mortgage loans for 1) construction or rehabilitation of nursing homes or intermediate care facilities, 2) nonprofit hospitals including moveable equipment, 3) group practice dentistry medicine or optometry.

Loans for land development must be applied for at FHA office for purchase of land and the development of building sites for subdivisions of new communities.

Flood and Civil Disorder Insurance is available to property owners and private insurers by applying at HUD central office.

It may be used for 1) flood insurance in flood-prone areas or, 2) urban property protection and reinsurance against losses from civil disorders.

HUD has a variety of programs which make special provisions for the victims of disasters. To apply contact FHA and HUD depending on the program.

> Dept. of Housing and Urban Development
> 451 Seventh St. S.W.
> Washington, D.C. 20410
> (202) 755-6420

Regional Office Housing and Urban Development

Region I	Address/Telephone
Massachusetts, New Hampshire, Maine, Rhode Island, Vermont, Connecticut	John F. Kennedy Federal Bldg. Boston, Massachusetts 02203 (617) 223-4066

Region II

New York, New Jersey	26 Federal Plaza New York, New York 10007 (212) 264-8068

Region III

Pennsylvania, Virginia, Washington, D.C., Maryland, West Virginia, Delaware	6th and Walnut Sts. Philadelphia, Pennsylvania 19106 (215) 597-2560

Region IV

Kentucky, Alabama, Florida, South Carolina, North Carolina, Mississippi, Tennessee, Georgia	1371 Peachtree St. N.E. Atlanta, Georgia 30309 (404) 526-5585

Region V	*Address/Telephone*
Michigan, Ohio, Wisconsin, Minnesota, Illinois, Indiana	300 South Wacker Dr. Chicago, Illinois 60606 (312) 353-5680
Region VI	
Louisiana, Arkansas, Texas, Oklahoma, New Mexico	1100 Commerce St. Dallas, Texas 75202 (214) 749-7401
Region VII	
Kansas, Missouri, Nebraska, Iowa	911 Walnut St. Kansas City, Missouri 64106 (816) 374-2661
Region VIII	
Colorado, Montana, North Dakota, South Dakota, Utah, Wyoming	1961 Stout St. Denver, Colorado 80202 (303) 837-4881
Region IX	
California, Hawaii, Nevada, Arizona	450 Golden Gate Ave. San Francisco, California 94102

Region X	Address/Telephone
Oregon, Washington, Idaho, Alaska	1321 2nd Ave. Seattle, Washington 98101 (206) 442-5415

CHAPTER XIV

In addition to the cash benefits and financial aid, the government also has some services and programs available to its citizens. These additional benefits are often available at no cost.

There are a number of educational exchange programs available; as well as, means of educating yourself in certain areas, through the U.S. Government programs. The Government can help you get a job, take a vacation or improve your business just to name a few.

These benefits are available to you now. Contact the necessary department of the government and take advantage of everything your government has to offer you.

COPYRIGHTS

In 1870 the United States was provided with protection for authors of artistic, dramatic, literary and musical works. This gives the author the exclusive right to copy, publish, adapt and record the work, (with some limitations).

Only an author or someone getting rights from the author can claim copyright to a work. A copyright lasts for 28 years and may be renewed for a second 28 year term.

Claims are registered and the copyright owner is mailed a certificate. The application and copies of the work are catalogued for the official records. Since 1897, over 11 million claims have been registered.

The duties of the copyright office include examination, registration, and cataloging of claims and supplying application forms and information. The office does not give legal advice. A court must decide whether or not there has been an infringement of the copyright.

Under the law, new versions may be copyrighted. "New works" include adaptions, abridgments, compilations, dramatizations, translations and arrangements. Copyright protection cannot be lengthened by republishing the work with new matter. Reprints will not be registered. Unless a new version is so different in substance from the original it will not be registered.

The Copyright Office considers only the information on the application when determining registerability. They do not compare versions of a work.

To be copyrightable, a work must be "the writing of an author".

If no authorship is involved, as in an abridgement or compilation, it may not be copyrighted.

There are fees for copyrighting a work. They should be paid by check or money order. For all classes of works, the fee for registration is $6.00. For renewal during the 28th year of the first term of copyright the fee is $4.00

For further information contact:
The Copyright Office
The Library of Congress
Washington, D.C. 20405

COUNSELING AND GUIDANCE TRAINING

The origin and purpose of this program was to make sure there would be enough manpower of quality and quantity to meet the needs of the U.S. defense system. Part of the National Defense Education Act authorizes the Commissioner of Education to improve the qualifications of personnel who guide and counsel students.

Accredited colleges or universities under contract with the U.S. Office of Education conduct a program for secondary school counselors or teachers preparing to become counselors. It is their aim to improve qualification and proficiency in the guidance and counseling of able secondary school students. Instruction is at the graduate level and is conducted in order to accelerate learning by those enrolled.

A "short term" institute is arranged a part of summer session, not less than four weeks in length. A regular session is part of a regular academic year either one semester or one quarter in length.

The Commissioner of Education decides which institutions to award contracts in National Defense Guidance and Counseling. A Registry form must be signed by the president or his representative (of the college or university).

Each institute has requirements for enrollment and they vary according to the program of each institute. Employees of elementary schools are not eligible. Enrollees must have at least a bachelor's degree. Some require even more education.

Academic credit and certification are not within the jurisdiction of the Office of Education. All institutions to date have granted credit upon completion of work. It is solely the institutions's responsibility.

CREDIT UNIONS

Under the U.S. Department of Health, Education and Welfare comes the Bureau of Federal Credit Unions. The Bureau provides a market for securities and makes credit available to people of small means. By setting up a national credit system of cooperative credit it helps stabilize the credit structure of the United States.

Offering a source of credit for productive purposes, they promote thrift among their members.

The Bureau of Federal Credit Unions, charters, examines, and supervises Federal Credit Unions.

There are more than ten thousand in operation.

Any group of 200 or more members may qualify for a charter. This includes rural communities of 200 families or 100 employees of one company.

The Bureau of Federal Credit Unions will help groups establish a credit union.

For more information contact:

Bureau of Federal Credit Unions
Social Security Administration
Washington, D.C. 20201

Region I	*Address*
Connecticut, Maine, Massachusetts, New Hampshire, Rhode Island, Vermont	Room 423 120 Boylston St. Boston, Mass.
Region II-A	
New York (except Long Island and State Island).	Room 1200 42 Broadway New York, N.Y.

174

Region II-B	Address
New Jersey, New York (Long Island and Staten Island only)	Room 1200 42 Broadway New York, N.Y.
Region II-C	
Delaware, Pennsylvania	Room 207, Blackston Bldg. 112 Market St. Harrisburg, Pa.
Region III	
District of Columbia, Kentucky, Maryland, North Carolina, Puerto Rico, Virginia, Virgin Islands, West Virginia	700 East Jefferson St. Charlottesville, Va.
Region IV	
Alabama, Canal Zone, Florida, Georgia, Mississippi, South Carolina, Tennesee	Room 404 50 - 7th Ave. NE Atlanta, Ga.
Region V	
Illinois, Indiana, Michigan, Ohio, Wisconsin	Room 712 433 West Van Buren St. Chicago, Ill

Region VI	Address
Colorado, Idaho, Iowa, Kansas, Minnesota, Missouri, Montana, Nebraska, North Dakota, South Dakota, Utah, Wyoming	Region 2302 Federal Office Bldg. 911 Walnut St. Kansas City, Mo.

Region VII

Arkansas, Louisiana, New Mexico, Oklahoma, Texas	1114 Commerce St. Dallas, Texas

Region VIII

Alaska, Arizona, California, Hawaii, Nevada, Oregon, Washington	Room 447 Federal Office Bldg. Civic Center San Francisco, Calif.

CULTURAL EXCHANGE

The State Department conducts cultural and educational exchange programs through the Bureau of Educational and Cultural Affairs. These are the different exchange programs offered.

1) Student exchange - Americans may do graduate studies in foreign countries and foreign students may come to student leader seminars and for educational travel to the United States.

2) Teacher exchange - Americans teach abroad in elementary and secondary schools. Foreign teachers and educators come to the United States to teach.

3) University Lecturers and Research Scholars Program - Through this program, American lecturers do advanced study abroad and lecture while foreign nationals do likewise in the U.S.A.

4) Foreign Leader Program - Foreigners who are leaders in government, politics and the arts are able to visit the United States.

5) Specialist Exchange - Specialists from America lecture, teach, advise or give performances abroad and foreign specialists do the same in the United States.

The Bureau of Educational and Cultural Exchange offers grants-in-aid to all of the following; 1) American sponsored schools abroad, 2) organizations and groups with youth programs, 3) colleges and universities in America that carry on junior year abroad projects and seminars for foreign student leaders, 4) organizations that sponsor projects in American studies in foreign countries.

CUSTOMS AUCTIONS

When people passing through customs do not pay the duties on the merchandise they are bringing through, the items are taken from them. The Customs Department holds auctions during the year in order to clear storehouses of these items.

Wholesalers, retailers as well as other consumers are welcome. In most cases items are viewed a day before the sale and may not be seen the day of the auction.

Merchandise for sale may include clothing, cars, cigarettes and liquor, all at low prices. For example, a car was purchased for less than half its domestic value.

Large quantities are available to wholesalers and retailers. Yard goods and jewelry are often among items for sale at auction. The largest customs auction is held in

New York City at U.S. Customs House, 201 Varick Street. You may attend an auction and just observe. What you purchase must be paid for in cash or by certified check.

Districts holding annual auctions may be obtained by writing and requesting a list from,

> The Bureau of Customs
> 2100 K Street N.W.
> Washington, D.C. 20226

FILMS AND EDUCATIONAL MEDIA
FOR THE DEAF

The Department of Health, Education and Welfare loans films with captions and other media for the education of the deaf. The service obtains films and film rights, equipment for captioning films and distribution facilities for educational equipment and material to State schools for the deaf and other agencies. Research and training in this area is also done by the service.

For more information:

> Director, Division of Education of the Deaf
> Office of Education
> Washington, D.C. 20201

SERVICES FOR THE DEAF

Captioned films are issued by the Department of Health, Education, and Welfare Division of Education Research.

In Washington, D.C., Gallaudet College was established to provide a source of higher education for the deaf. The Federal Government gives it extensive support.

The Veterans Administration helps with vocational rehabilitation, medical care, and special equipment.

The address of Gallaudet College is

> Gallaudet College
> Seventh St. and Florida Ave. NE
> Washington, D.C.

EDUCATIONAL AND CULTURAL AFFAIRS

The Bureau of Educational and Cultural Affairs conducts programs which send athletes and artists who perform, overseas. People come to the United States for experience, observation and travel.

American - sponsored schools in Latin America and other areas receive grants and special services through programs administered through this Bureau.

Exchange programs that further the national interest

may receive aid. For more information contact;

Bureau of Educational and Cultural Affairs
U.S. Department of State
Washington, D.C.

HEAD START

Children who are deprived of normal exposure to books at an early age may attend story hours at their public libraries. Funds to support this program are provided through the Library Services and Construction Act. The funds may be used for organization, library materials, publicity and staffing.

The aim of the Head Start Program is to raise the learning capacity of children 3 to 5 years of age to a higher level before they enter school. Parents interested in this program should inquire at their library.

Those interested in beginning a Head Start Program in their community should write to the Office of Education in their state to the Library Extension Division.

HOMESTEADING

Early in the history of the United States the western part of the country was unexplored. When gold was discovered in 1849 in California, many new people moved to the West. Although they did not find gold, many stayed on to farm or raise cattle. From the time of President Jefferson new territories were added to the United States. In 1867 Russia sold Alaska to the U.S. for seven million dollars.

All these territories became part of the property owned by the American people. The United States then became responsible for taking care of them. This property is called public domain.

Also, in the early days of this country, the government encouraged people to settle in these undeveloped areas. They wanted them to build homes and later obtain ownership of the land. Large numbers of people were able to do this because of the Homestead Act. The Homestead Act was passed in 1862 by Congress. It is still in effect today.

In order to be eligible, any U.S. citizen 21 years of age may settle on public domain land. In order to own the land, he must build a home and live on the land for five years.

At present, there are 720 million acres of land in the public domain. Nearly all of Alaska is still public domain. There is none in Hawaii. Some homesteading is still going on in Alaska, where there is quite a lot of farmland. It is an opportunity for the future!

In 1938, Congress made it possible for anyone to obtain 3 to 5 acres on which to build a vacation or permanent home. This law makes it possible for a man to become owner of the land even if he does not live in the home on the land. The land is no longer free. At times they are sold for several hundred dollars.

For more information contact the Bureau of Land Management.

PHYSICAL FITNESS

The Presidents Council on Physical Fitness has a great deal of literature available. The aim of the Council is to improve the physical fitness of the general population. They can help individuals and communities to improve facilities for physical education for school age children. The Council will help you set up a Community Committee on Physical Fitness. For more information, write:

> The President's Council on Physical Fitness
> Room 4830
> General Accounting Building
> Washington, D.C. 20001

AMERICAN PRINTING HOUSE
FOR THE BLIND

This printing house is located in Louisville, Kentucky. Books and teaching materials are manufactured and distributed to educational institutions for the blind. Braille books, Talking books, Braille music, large type books, educational tape recordings and other tangible apparatus for the blind are issued through this printing house.

In 1879 a Federal Act "To Promote the Education of the Blind" was authorized for the support of the Printing House. Originally, the money was available only to furnish instructional aids for students in public schools for the blind or specially organized classes for the blind in public schools. An amendment, in 1956 extended the benefits. Now all blind students can benefit, regardless of whether or not they are enrolled in classes exclusively for the blind.

Congress appropriates funds for the Printing House to the U.S. Department of Health, Education and Welfare. The U.S. Treasury Department transfers the funds to the Printing House which allocates specific amounts to various superintendents of schools for the blind or chief state school officers. They receive money in shares directly proportionate to the numbers of blind students enrolled in the school. Books and materials are then shipped to the schools against the funds credited them by the government. The Printing House may not use Federal funds to build or lease buildings.

In 1966, an amendment was passed by Congress extending coverage to include handicapped people, such as those with paralysis, who cannot read books.

More information is available from:

> Director, Office of Financial Management
> Department of Health, Education and Welfare
> Washington, D.C.

Business Reference Library. By writing, calling or visiting the Small Business Administration, businessmen and SBA Counselors may use the reference library in Washington or the larger field offices. Textbooks, Government and private publications on management and other helpful topics are available.

A list of regional offices is included at the end of Chapter XI The Small Business Administration.

Business Management and Research. Technical and managerial help is available to small business firms.

Advice and counseling on policies, principles and good management practices. The Small Business Administration cooperates with business and educational, professional and other non-profit organizations. It also acts as a clearinghouse and distribution center for information about finance, management and operation of small businesses. Management skills can be developed.

The small business owner needs this help to interpret facts enabling them to become more successful.

They can find out what they need to know to compete with businesses that are older, richer or bigger.

A small business man is unable to hire consultants or specialists on management methods for financial reasons. In most cases, such experts are expensive.

Our economy needs the small businessman to keep it "healthy."Small business enterprises help lessen economic and political control, and diversify employment opportunities. New products as well as, new methods of production are often developed by small firms. This, in addition to, keeping prices reasonable is all possible because of the individual business man.

The Small Business Administration helps owners of small businesses to help themselves. In this day and age, owners of small firms must be well informed. With the information and ability to apply it, a businessman is able to make the decisions necessary to make his enterprise a success.

There are many management assistance programs that offer help not available from other sources. The government does this because it believes in small businesses. They are vital to our economy. The SBA helps strengthen them by providing management and research assistance.

Each week hundreds of businessmen make use of these programs either in Washington or at the various field offices for individual assistance.

There are also reference libraries. A special business library in Washington has been set up. There are similar libraries in selected SBA regional offices, although they are not so extensive. Included in the reference libraries are textbooks, handbooks, magazines, booklets, leaflets, business papers, and rosters of special assistance groups.

A program to promote customer-supplier relations is another part of the agency's counseling service. Large businesses realize that it is in their own self-interest to help small customers and suppliers to improve their management. Customers who are better managed sell more and pay bills faster. Deliveries are also faster and more dependable. The SBA encourages large and medium sized businesses to aid small firms.

There are educational programs, courses and conferences to strengthen small firms, and their owners. Administrative management courses are co-sponsored by public and private institutions and the SBA. Courses on planning, organizing, and directing are offered. Financial responsibility rests on the educational institution and the businessmen who pay a fee to attend the courses. Research is also conducted by the SBA to learn about improved teaching methods.

The National Council for Small Business Management Development which is made up of representatives of educational institutions who have conducted courses co-ponsored by the SBA. Televised courses are available in many communities

During the first eight years of this program, 1500 courses were co-sponsored by the SBA and 500 educational institutions. About 50,000 owners and managers of small business attended these courses. Today, the number of courses, institutions, and businessmen attending them has increased.

Conferences on taxes, exports, and management are held to aid the small businessman. There is a wealth of information available for your use if you own or operate a small business or intend to start a business of your own. Contact your regional office of the SBA they can direct you to the proper channels.

Campground Development. There are two types of campgrounds; travelers' campground and vacation campgrounds. Travelers campgrounds are used by travelers as overnight stops when they are en route to a certain destination, while vacation campgrounds are the destination itself. Vacation campgrounds provide more facilities for recreation, eating and sleeping.

The government will aid you in developing a campground as a full time business or as a supplement to an already established business. For example, if you own timberland you might use a portion of the wooded land as lots for campers.

State and local agencies can give assistance in developing the land. Here are several commissions and departments you might contact for help.

> Conservation Service
> Forestry Service

Dept. of Health, Education and Welfare
U.S. Travel Service
Fish and Game Commission

Before beginning a camping trip write the Forest Service of the particular National forest you intend to visit and they will send you a guide indicating major recreational areas.

There are approximately 186 million acres of National forests and grasslands that campers enjoy each year. Fishing streams and natural lakes are available for their use. The streams total 81,000 miles and the lakes cover about 3 million acres.

Almost everyone can drive to a Forest Service campground in a day. Nearly every major highway in the Nation passes through one or more National Forests.

There are some basic things all campgrounds have in common, although no two campgrounds are exactly alike. Some of the basics included are; camping units about 100 ft. apart, a place to park, firegrate, trash cans, drinking water, tables and benches, and a latrine. Grounds with fields and meadows have cleared places for tents.

Here are some frequently asked questions concerning camping in National Forests.

Question: What is the camping season?

Answer: The regular season is usually from May 30th through Labor Day weekend. If the ground is located in a warmer climate it may be extended, or all year round.

Question: Must you make reservations?

Answer: Campsites are filled on a first come, first serve basis.

Question: What does it cost?

Answer: In almost all National Forests, camping is free. There are a few special service areas where a charge of 50 cents to $1.00 per person per day is charged.

Question: How long can you stay?

Answer: The most popular areas limit you to 2 weeks, but in most cases you may visit as long as you like. ·

Question: What equipment is needed?

Answer: Your own tent, sleeping gear, and cooking equipment as well as food.

Question: What are the rules regarding trailers?

Answer: In most cases, water, electrical and sewage connections are not provided; and waste water is not allowed to drain on the grounds. Many offer separate trailer accommodations, some are commercially operated. Small trailers may be used where parking space is large enough for both car and trailer.

Question: What rules apply to campfires and cooking?

Answer: Fires may be built at campgrounds and other sites designated without a permit. In California a permit is needed; also, in wilderness areas, the Forest Rangers should be contacted to check requirements. Campers are not allowed to cut standing timber, bushes or other vegetation.

Question: What about water or supplies?

Answer: Most campgrounds have safe drinking water available. Concessioners may supply hot water and laundry facilities. Supplies such as milk, ice and other provisions are available in nearby towns or from concessioners.

Question: Are there rules about pets?

Answer: Yes, they are subject to state laws which vary. In some states dogs must be kept on a leash.

Question: Are there rules regarding firearms?

Answer: Yes, firearms are subject to state laws. They are prohibited in State and Federal game refuges.

According to one government source it would take a life time year round camping, if a week were spent at each campground.

These beautiful sites and areas are available to all of us for hiking, fishing, camping, and water sports just to name a few.

For more information on National Forests and National Grasslands write the appropriate forrester in your region. The addresses are in the following directory.

Region I	*Address*
Massachusetts, New Hampshire, Maine, Rhode Island, Vermont, Connecticut	Federal Building Missoula, Mont.

Region II

New York, New Jersey	Federal Center, Building 35 Denver Colo.

Region III

Pennsylvania, Virginia, Washington, D.C., Maryland, West Virginia, Delaware	517 Gold Street S.W. Albuquerque, New Mexico

Region IV

Kentucky, Alabama, Florida, South Carolina, North Carolina, Mississippi, Tennessee, Georgia	Forest Service Building Ogden, Utah

Region V

Michigan, Ohio, Wisconsin, Minnesota, Illinois, Indiana	630 Sansome Street San Francisco, California

Region VI

Louisiana, Arkansas,
Texas, Oklahoma,
New Mexico

Post Office Box 4137
Portland, Oregon

Region VII

Kansas, Missouri,
Nebraska, Iowa

6816 Market St.
Upper Darby, Pa.

Region VIII

Colorado, Montana,
North Dakota, South
Dakota, Utah,
Wyoming

50 Seventh St.
Atlanta, Georgia

Region IX

California, Hawaii,
Nevada, Arizona

710 N. 6th St.
Milwaukee, Wis.

Region X

Oregon, Washington,
Idaho, Alaska

Fifth Street
Office Building
Post Office Box 1631
Juneau, Alaska

Christmas trees. The Bureau of Land Management, for a fee will grant you a permit to cut your own Christmas tree from Western public lands.

In Las Vegas alone about 1500 families cut their own tree. The cutting area is not near population centers so people traveled 175 miles to cut their own tree.

Pine and juniper are the most plentiful and they must be at least 3 ft. tall to be cut. For a permit write the Bureau of Land Management Land offices listed in this directory.

BUREAU OF LAND MANAGEMENT
LAND OFFICES

555 Cordova Street
Anchorage, Alaska 99501

516 Second Avenue
Fairbanks, Alaska 99701

Federal Building, Room 204
Phoenix, Arizona 85025

Federal Building, Room 4017
Sacramento, California 95814

1414 8th Street
Riverside, California 92502

BUREAU OF LAND MANAGEMENT
LAND OFFICES (Cont.)

700 Gas & Electric Building
Denver, Colorado 80202

323 Federal Building
Boise, Idaho 83701

Federal Building
316 N. 26th Street
Billings, Montana 59101
(Covers North and South Dakota also)

560 Mill Street
Reno, Nevada 89505

Federal Building
Santa Fe, New Mexico 87501
(Covers Oklahoma also)

710 NE. Holladay
Portland, Oregon 97232

Third Floor, Federal Building
125 South State Street
P.O. Box 11505
Salt Lake City, Utah 84110

BUREAU OF LAND MANAGEMENT
LAND OFFICES (continued)

670 Bon Marche Building
Spokane, Washington 99201

2002 Capitol Avenue
Cheyenne, Wyoming
(Covers Nebraska and Kansas also)

La Salle Building
1728 L St. NW.
Washington, D.C. 20240
(Covers all other states also)

Civil Service. You can get a job working for the Federal Government. At this time, over two and a half million are employed by the U.S. Government. They work at offices, laboratories, hospitals, machine shops, and delivering mail. They protect us, maintain our parks, inspect our food, and forecast the weather. About one tenth of those employed by the Federal Government, work in Washington. Jobs discussed in this section are those under the civil service merit system, such as, Post Office Department or the Federal Aviation Agency, and others in the executive branch of the government.

Appointments to jobs under this system are made on the basis of ability to do the work. This is determined by examinations. There is no prejudice. All applicants receive equal consideration. The positions are called "competitive" because applicants compete for them in civil service examinations. These are the jobs discussed in this section.

THE CIVIL SERVICE COMMISSION

This Federal Agency has a central office in Washington. Outside Washington, work is carried on through regional offices. They give examinations and fill positions as well as supply civil service information.

All types of jobs are available with the government but the Civil Service Commission doesn't accept all kinds of jobs all the time. Jobs must be available before they will open an exam and accept applications. When a job exists an announcement is made telling about the job and what education and experience is needed.

Boards of the U.S. Civil Service Examiners are maintained in post offices. These offices can supply you with information and application forms. If you do not meet the requirements in the application you should not file an application.

These are some of the general requirements that must be met: 1) Usually age must be at least 18 years, there is no maximum. If the minimum age is different the announcement will specify; 2) Only citizens of the U.S. may take examinations; 3) You must be physically able to perform the duties of the position for which you apply. This does not disqualify the physically handicapped. If there are special physical requirements, they will be described in the announcement.

The next step is filling out an application. They are usually 2 to 4 pages long and must be filled out carefully and completely. If each question is not answered the Civil

Service will have to write for the information and that takes time. If you do not reply quickly your application will not be accepted.

In some cases there are no written tests so you should tell all you can about your experience and training.

Examinations given will test either your ability to do the job or the ability to learn to do the job.

If you fail you may take it again. If you pass, but want to improve your score a year must pass before you can retake it (provided the examination is still open).

Applicants will be notified by the office that announced the examination. Those who pass are called eligibles. The higher your score the better your chance. The top three people who fit the requirements are sent to the Commission. Appointments are made from those three names by an officer. The other names are put back on the list to be considered for future openings. Veterans get preference.

There are different kinds of appointments which are temporary, career conditional, or careeer. Temporary appointments do not last more than one year. If an applicant is over 70 years old, this is the only type of appointment that can be given but it may be renewed. Temporary workers are not under the retirement system and may not be promoted or transferred. Career-conditional appointments are three years in length and leads to a career appointment. The first year is a probationary period. A career employee has transfer and promotion privileges. His group is the last to be affected by layoffs.

There are other requirements, besides ability to do the work. 1) Sometimes proof must be supplied showing that they meet a one year residence requirement. 2) 2 or more members of a family living under the same roof may not hold Federal jobs. 3) Appointee must be able to swear to the truth of certain statements. 4) He must also take an Oath of Office to defend and support the constitution. 5) He must swear that he is not a Communist or Fascist and does not advocate the overthrow of the U.S. Government. 6) He must swear that he will not strike against the government. 7) He must swear that he did not bribe anyone to get his job. 8) If he holds a State, City, or County job he may not keep it while he is a Federal employee. 9) The government will investigate him. 10) If his job requires that he travel to report for duty he must, in most cases, pay his own way. 11) He must pass a physical examination. 12) His fingerprints will be taken. 12) While he is a Federal employee, he may not take an active part in politics.

The work week is usually 40 hours, 8 per day, 5 days per week. Vacation and sick leave is 13 days per year the first three years and 20 days for the next 12 years. After 15 years they get 26 days of leave. Sick leave is 13 days per year.

Civil Service Regional Offices

Region I	*Address*
Massachusetts, New Hampshire, Maine, Rhode Island, Vermont, Connecticut	John W. McCormack Post Office and Courthouse Boston, Massachusetts 02109 (617) 223-2538

Region II	
New York, New Jersey	26 Federal Plaza New York, New York 10007 (212) 264-0440

Region III	
Pennsylvania, West Virginia, Washington, D.C., Maryland, West Virginia, Delaware	600 Arch St. Philadelphia, Pennsylvania 19106 (215) 597-4543

Region IV

Kentucky, Alabama, Florida, South Carolina, North Carolina, Mississippi, Tennessee, Georgia	1340 Spring St. N.W. Atlanta, Georgia 30309 (404) 526-2436

Region V

Michigan, Ohio, Wisconsin, Minnesota, Illinois, Indiana	230 South Dearborn St. Chicago, Illinois 60604 (312) 353-2901

Region VI

Louisiana, Arkansas, Texas, Oklahoma, New Mexico	1100 Commerce St. Dallas, Texas 75202 (214) 749-3352

Region VII

Kansas, Missouri, Nebraska, Iowa	1520 Market St. St. Louis, Missouri 63103 (314) 622-4262

Region VIII

Colorado, Montana, North Dakota, South Dakota, Utah Wyoming	Denver Federal Center Bldg. 20 Denver, Colorado 80225 (303) 234-2023

Region IX

California, Hawaii,
Nevada, Arizona

450 Golden Gate Ave.
San Francisco, California
94102
(415) 556-0581

Region X

Oregon, Washington,
Idaho, Alaska

915 2nd Ave.
Seattle, Washington 98174
(206) 442-7536

Coast and Geodetic Survey. This agency of the U.S. Department of Commerce provides charts and other information for safe navigation of water or air commerce. The division of technical and administrative services publishes most of the technical information. Its library contains about 130,000 books and 500 journals, some dating back as far as the 19th century. Such subjects as oceanography, cartography and photogammetry are included. On site reference use is limited to graduate students and other agencies of the government. The geographic branch provides maps and charts some of which are on microfilm. They also have a Visual Aids Sections with a collection of still and panchromatic photographs and motion pictures showing the Coast and

Geodetic Survey activities.

Private industry and universities are eligible for research grants from this office.

Leaflets, brochures and pamphlets about the activities of the office are available.

The headquarters office is:

> Coast and Geodetic Survey
> U.S. Department of Commerce
> Washington, D.C. 20230

Publications, motion pictures, maps, charts and other data are available for loan or sale through the regional offices at the following addresses:

> U.S. Coast and Geodetic Survey
>
> Room 535
> 417 South Hill Street
> Los Angeles, California 90013
>
> Room 121, Customhouse
> 555 Battery Street
> San Francisco, California 94111
>
> Post Office Box 190
> 19th and Grant Streets
> Tampa, Florida 33601

Room 224, Federal Building
Post Office Box 3887
Honolulu, Hawaii 96812

Room 314, U.S. Courthouse
Portland, Maine 04105

10th Floor, Courthouse
Boston, Massachusetts 02109

Room 2603, Federal Building
911 Walnut Street
Kansas City, Missouri 64106

Room 221, University Plaza
100 North University Drive
Fort Worth, Texas 76107

102 Olney Road
Norfolk, Virginia 23510

Room 602, Federal Building
90 Church Street
New York, New York 10007

Room 705, Federal Building
Seattle, Washington 98104

Room 315 Customhouse
423 Canal Street
New Orleans, Louisiana 70130

BIBLIOGRAPHY

Dolmatch, T.B., editor, *Information-Please Almanac,* New York: Information Please Publishing, Inc., 1978.

Grisham, R.A., Jr., and McConaughy, P.D., editors, *Encyclopedia of U.S. Government Benefits,* New Jersey: William H. Wise and Company, 1973.

O'Connor, Patricia, editor, *Washington Information Directory,* Washington, D.C., Congressional Quarterly, 1975-6.

Ruder, William and Nathan, R., *The Businessman's Guide to Washington,* New York, Macmillan Publishing Company, Inc., 1975.

Prepared by editors of Encyclopedia Britannica, *The U.S. Government: How and Why It Works,* New York: Bantam Books, Inc., 1978.

Social Security and Medicare Explained, Chicago, Illinois: Commerce Clearing House, 1977.

Pamphlets: U.S. Government Printing Office, 1977

"If You Work After You Retire"

"If You Become Disabled"

"Estimating Your Social Security Check"

"SSI For The Aged, Blind, and Disabled"

"Your 1978 Social Security Deduction"

"Your Social Security"

"When You Work At A Job"